DANIEL: STANDING FIRM IN ADVERSITY

Paul S. Kim

STUDY GUIDE WITH LEADER'S NOTES

newgrowthpress.com

New Growth Press, Greensboro, NC 27401
newgrowthpress.com

Cover Design: Faceout Studio, faceoutstudio.com
Interior Typesetting and Ebook: Lisa Parnell, lparnellbookservices.com
Exercises and Application Questions: Kristen J. Hsu

ISBN: 978-1-64507-507-3 (print)
ISBN: 978-1-64507-508-0 (ebook)

Printed in the United States of America

29 28 27 26 25 1 2 3 4 5

CONTENTS

INTRODUCTION

All of us face adversity. This Bible study on the book of Daniel explores how to stand firm in the midst of it. Daniel, an Old Testament prophet, was an exile living in Babylon where he faced challenges and pressures to conform to the ways of the world. Like Daniel, Christians today live in the world as exiles. In the New Testament, the apostle Peter writes to followers of Jesus scattered throughout Asia Minor, calling them "sojourners and exiles" (1 Peter 2:11), and he refers to these last days as "Babylon" (1 Peter 5:13).

So, while the book of Daniel is an ancient book written many centuries ago, its context and message are very relevant to our time today!

How was Daniel able to live such a life of conviction without compromise? How was he able to thrive and not simply survive the Christian life in a world of persecution and pressure? How was he able to worship the Lord in Babylon and not grow angry and bitter toward God and the people living in Babylon?

In Daniel, we see a portrait of deep biblical faith that enabled him to stand firm in adversity. And as we will see, the focus is not on Daniel as an example but as a pointer to the true and greater Daniel, Jesus.

It is deeply comforting to know that Jesus, the greater Daniel, understands all the challenges, sufferings, and hardships God's people face in exile today. But even more, Jesus entered our world of exile, suffering to put an end to all suffering. Jesus lived the perfect, righteous life, not as a moral example but as our substitute and righteousness. And Jesus entered our world of exile with the specific purpose of bringing us home. Life will not end for us as captives in Babylon but as God's children in the new heaven and earth that will last forever (Revelation 21:1)!

It is with Christ's suffering, death, resurrection, and future homecoming in mind that followers of Jesus can stand firm in adversity as exiles today. Not only that, God's people are called to bless those in Babylon.

The prophet Jeremiah, a contemporary of Daniel's, spoke to those living in Babylon with surprising instructions for how they should live:

> "Thus says the Lord of hosts, the God of Israel, to all the exiles whom I have sent into exile from Jerusalem to Babylon: Build houses and live in them; plant gardens and eat their produce. Take wives and have sons and daughters . . . multiply there, and do not decrease. But seek the welfare of the city where I have sent you into exile, and pray to the Lord on its behalf, for in its welfare you will find your welfare." (Jeremiah 29:4–7)

May the gospel cause us to do the same today.

HISTORICAL BACKGROUND

First of all, who is Daniel? Daniel is an Old Testament prophet to Israel's Southern Kingdom, during a unique time in the history of God's people in the Old Testament.

Figure 1: Timeline of Daniel[1]

DATE (approximate)	EVENT
1050 BC	Israel becomes a kingdom.
1000 BC	The kingdom of Israel reaches its pinnacle when David becomes king.
970 BC	David's son Solomon becomes the king. Solomon's heart begins to turn from the Lord, and after Solomon's death, the kingdom of Israel is divided between the Northern Kingdom of Israel and the Southern Kingdom of Judah. During this tumultuous period of the kings, there are a few bright moments when God's people turn from idolatry, but there is an overall spiritual decline that leads to the eventual fall of both kingdoms.
722 BC	The Northern Kingdom of Israel falls to Assyria.
605 BC	Daniel is taken into exile in Babylon.
586 BC	The Southern Kingdom of Judah falls to Babylon, which leads to seventy years of exile for God's people. During this time of exile, the Lord raises up Daniel to be a prophet to his people in Babylon.

Israel first became a kingdom around 1050 BC. A little later, at the pinnacle of David's and Solomon's rule, God's people were to be a witness to the world of what it means to have God, the Creator and Redeemer, at the center of their lives. Unfortunately, they repeatedly rejected God and turned away from him to worship idols. Eventually their sin led to Israel splitting into a Northern Kingdom and a Southern Kingdom. The Northern Kingdom was conquered by Assyria around 722 BC. The Southern Kingdom continued for a little while longer but eventually fell to the nation of Babylon. Around 605 BC, Daniel was among the first group of key leaders who were sent into

1. Dates and historical information for this timeline are drawn from Lane T. Dennis and Wayne Grudem, eds., *ESV Study Bible* (Crossway, 2008), 508, 543, 599, 782, 797, 1581.

exile in Babylon. Several decades later (around 586 BC), the Southern Kingdom was defeated by Babylon: Jerusalem was sacked, the temple was destroyed, and many captives were sent to Babylon as exiles.

Despite punishing them for their sin, God had not abandoned his people. After they had spent seventy years in Babylon, which had in turn been conquered by the Persians, God moved in the hearts of Israel's captors to let them return to Jerusalem and rebuild. (The books of Ezra and Nehemiah tell this part of God's story.) Daniel's ministry is a stark reminder that even in the midst of dark times and uncertainty, God's purposes cannot be thwarted, and his covenant love for his people cannot be exhausted.

LITERARY STRUCTURE OF DANIEL

There are two ways to view the structure of the book of Daniel. The first is to see the twelve chapters as divided into two parts:

Figure 2: The Two Parts of Daniel

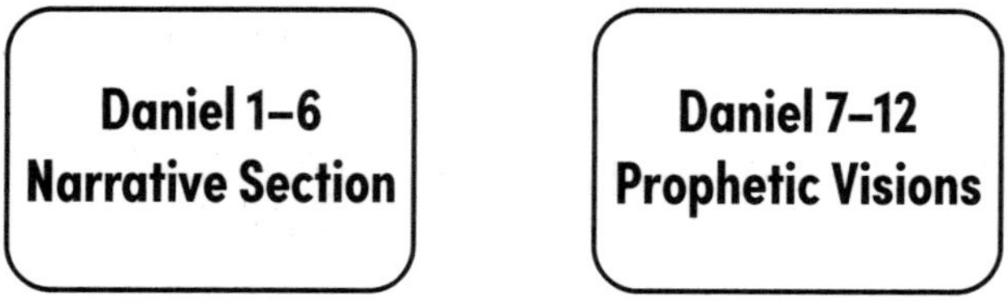

Daniel 1–6 Narrative Section	Daniel 7–12 Prophetic Visions

- **Chapters 1–6: Narrative section.** It contains the well-known stories of Daniel in the lion's den and Daniel's friends in the fiery furnace.
- **Chapters 7–12: Apocalyptic prophetic visions.** These visions are quite intense, and while readers may wonder what they are all about, the big picture is that they are speaking about what will take place beyond exile.

The second way of looking at the structure of Daniel is more complex:

Figure 3: The Structure of Daniel by Language and Theme

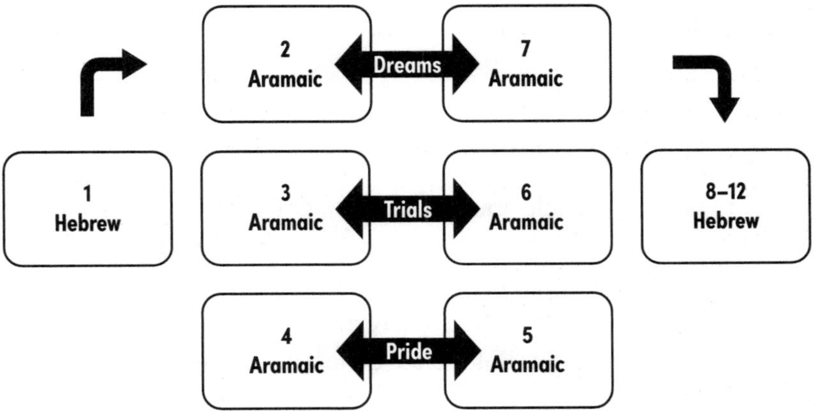

2 Aramaic — Dreams — 7 Aramaic
1 Hebrew
3 Aramaic — Trials — 6 Aramaic
8–12 Hebrew
4 Aramaic — Pride — 5 Aramaic

The book of Daniel was originally written in two languages.

Hebrew is the language used for the introduction (chapter 1) and the conclusion (chapters 8–12). Aramaic is used for chapters 2–7.

Notice the pairs in the Aramaic section (chapters 2–7):

- Chapters 2 and 7 consist of dreams about what's beyond exile, and it's a call to be faithful, even in the midst of the uncertainty of the future.
- Chapters 3 and 6 are about trials. Chapter 3 is the account of Daniel's friends in the fiery furnace, and chapter 6 gives the account of Daniel in the lion's den. These chapters tell us that life in exile may consist of suffering and hardship, but God's people can take heart because God is with them.
- Chapters 4 and 5 are on the theme of pride. In chapter 4, King Nebuchadnezzar proudly declares his own might and authority as king of Babylon and he is humbled by God. In chapter 5,

> his son has essentially the same attitude and is also humbled by God. These chapters demonstrate that "God opposes the proud but gives grace to the humble" (James 4:6).

With context and structure in mind, let's jump into our study of Daniel.

HOW TO USE THIS STUDY

This study guide will help you learn from Daniel within a small group. Like Daniel, we are living in exile and are called to stand firm in adversity. Navigating life in a place that is not our true home is difficult. Try to make your group a place where everyone can be honest about the challenges of living in Babylon as exiles instead of pretending that life on earth is easy.

Each participant should have one of these study guides in order to join in reading and be able to work through the exercises during that part of the study. The study leader should read through both the lesson and the leader's notes in the back of this book before each lesson begins. No other preparation or homework is required.

There are ten lessons in this study guide. Each will take about an hour to complete, perhaps a bit more if your group is large, and will include these elements:

BIG IDEA. This is a summary of the main point of the lesson.

BIBLE CONVERSATION. The purpose of the Bible Conversation is to get the group to read the Bible passage together, look at it closely, think about it, and discuss it.

ARTICLE. This is the main teaching section of the lesson.

DISCUSSION. The discussion questions following the article will help you apply the teaching to your life.

EXERCISE. The exercise is a section you will complete on your own during group time. You can write in the book if that helps you. You will then share some of what you have learned with the group. If the group is large, it may help to split up to share the results of the exercise and to pray, so that everyone has a better opportunity to participate.

WRAP-UP AND PRAYER. God is a part of your conversation. He will speak to you through the Bible, and you will speak to him in prayer. Make this a much-anticipated element of the group dialogue.

As we learn about Daniel, we will see connections to our own lives and how Jesus is the true and greater Daniel—he endured exile on our behalf, is with us even now in our exile, and will one day take us out of exile to our eternal home.

Lesson

1

THE EXILE

BIG IDEA

The land of exile seeks to influence and shape you. Living by faith in exile means living by God's Word and the promises of the gospel.

BIBLE CONVERSATION *20 MINUTES*

First of all, who is Daniel? Daniel is an Old Testament prophet in Israel's Southern Kingdom of Judah during the tumultuous time when the nation of Babylon defeats Judah and takes God's people into exile.

Daniel was taken to Babylon in the first wave of the exile, which took place around 605 BC, before the fall of Jerusalem. In this first wave, the Babylonians took the cream of the crop, all the influencers. The idea was to have them formed and shaped by the culture of Babylon, to form a Babylonian identity within them.

The Bible tells us that all of us are living in exile today.[1] We are "banished" from God's home and presence because of sin. We can use the term *Babylon* to describe this life in exile, where people are captive to the shaping influences of sin. Such influence comes by way of the world, the flesh, and the devil.[2] Often, these influences put pressure

1. 1 Peter 1:1
2. Ephesians 2:1–3

on us to conform to this world out of fear or compromise. But in Daniel, we see a portrait of biblical faith that stands firm in adversity.

Have someone read **Daniel chapter 1** aloud, or have a few readers take turns. Then discuss the questions below:

Consider all that Daniel lost or left behind when he was forced into exile in Babylon (vv. 1–7). What would it be like to experience that?

In verses 8–21, we begin to see what living by faith in exile looks like for Daniel. What stands out to you? What questions do you have?

Daniel was removed from his land, his community, his culture, and the center of worship, yet God had not abandoned Daniel. Where do you see glimpses of God's presence with Daniel in exile?

****

Next, read this lesson's article. Take turns reading it aloud, switching readers at each paragraph break. Then discuss the questions that follow.

Lesson

LIVING BY FAITH IN EXILE

5 MINUTES

BABYLON: THE LAND OF EXILE

Daniel is taken in exile to Babylon, a foreign land and culture that is hostile to his faith. There's historical significance to Shinar, the place mentioned in verse 2. It's a place of power and pride, where back in Genesis 11, people declared their independence and built the Tower of Babel to become like God. This is where humanity opposed God, saying, "We're the masters of the universe."

Saint Augustine provides a helpful way to think about Babylon as the "City of Man," which stands in contrast to the "City of God." In his book *The City of God*, Augustine says that the City of Man is characterized by "love of self," whereas the City of God consists of people characterized by "love of God."[3] Babylon is the City of Man, characterized by power, pride, and pleasure. But the City of God, established by Jesus,[4] is characterized by "righteousness and peace and joy in the Holy Spirit" (Romans 14:17).

---

3. Saint Augustine, *The City of God* (Penguin Classics, 2003), 593.
4. Mark 1:15; Hebrews 12:22

BABYLON'S SHAPING INFLUENCES

Consider what it's like to live in such a place as Babylon, or the City of Man. None of us live in a vacuum; we are all immersed in a culture. Culture is always present—it's in the air that we breathe. Often, we are not aware of it, even though we are being shaped by it. Babylon was actively seeking to shape Daniel through its literature, language, and lifestyle. The same shaping forces are in place now—you and I are immersed in the literature, language (social media, what you hear in the news, the way you converse with people), and lifestyle of the surrounding culture.

The shaping influences of Babylon are so powerful because they seek to form and shape our core identity. Notice that Daniel and his friends had their names changed (v. 7). Why the change of names?

In the Bible, names are meaningful, and they often represent something significant about a person. The original names of Daniel and his friends were linked to God's nature and character, revealing something about their own sense of identity and personhood:

- *Daniel* meant "Elohim, God is my judge."[5]
- *Hananiah* meant "Yahweh is gracious."
- *Mishael* meant "Who is like Elohim?"
- *Azariah* meant "Yahweh helps."

In Babylon, their names are changed as a way to change their core identity. Today, your name might not be changed, but make no mistake: Babylon seeks to change and reshape your identity! The powerful influences of the world tempt God's people to forget their identity as children of God and instead find an identity in something other than the gospel in order to get meaning and purpose in life.

---

5. The translations in this list are taken from *All the Names in the Bible* (Thomas Nelson, 2014), 85, 161, 265, 489.

LIVING BY FAITH IN EXILE

Daniel lived by faith in God. This is remarkable because he was taken out of his home country into exile, where he lived in an environment that greatly pressured him to compromise his faith. Daniel was surrounded by a culture that did not know God and tempted him to reject God and follow the ways of the world.

What does it look like to live in a world that's trying to lure and pressure you to compromise your faith? How can you live by faith in God and stand firm through adversity?

Daniel points a way forward—he points to living by faith, and he points to Christ.

BY FAITH, DANIEL LIVED BY GOD'S WORD

We see Daniel's faith in action in verse 8, when he "resolved that he would not defile himself with the king's food, or with the wine that he drank." This may have been to keep biblical dietary laws or avoid food offered up to idols as a way to honor God and obey his Word. Or it may have been an act of bold faith, where Daniel takes a stand against the temptations and pleasures that the world offers and instead finds his satisfaction in God alone.

Here we see one way Daniel points us to Jesus. In his wilderness exile, after a forty-day fast, Jesus is tempted by the devil to turn stones into bread. Jesus resists temptation by quoting Scripture: "Man shall not live by bread alone, but by every word that comes from the mouth of God" (Matthew 4:4).

Living by faith in exile means living by God's Word. His Word satisfies our soul, and we are able to "taste and see that the Lord is good"

(Psalm 34:8). God's Word also brings conviction and enables us to fight temptation and sin.[6]

What's truly amazing is that God's Word IS a person! The apostle John tells us that "the Word became flesh and dwelt among us" (John 1:14). As the living Word, Jesus declares that he is "the bread of life" (John 6:35). Jesus is the One who truly satisfies our deepest hunger and longings.

BY FAITH, DANIEL LIVED WITH INTEGRITY

In Babylon, Daniel understood who he was: he was God's child and part of God's family. Even though he was living in Babylon and tempted by its power and influence, his identity was secure in his relationship with God. As a result, he wasn't trying to compromise, blend in, or please people. Instead, Daniel sought to please God. He did what he believed God wanted him to do, without knowing what the outcome of his actions would be. When he refused to eat the king's food, he risked punishment and rejection. Daniel didn't know if he would find favor with the chief of the eunuchs (v. 9) or the king (v. 20). But because he lived by faith in exile, secure in his Father's love, Daniel lived his life with gospel integrity.

DANIEL POINTS TO CHRIST

It can be easy to think, *Just do what Daniel did, live how Daniel lived.* However, such an approach will lead to pride or despair. Pride often leads to anger and bitterness, especially when we think that God ought to bless us because of our obedience. Despair comes about when we wilt under the pressure of Babylon and succumb to our fears. Our failures paralyze us and we lose all hope.

---

6. Psalm 119:11

But the good news is that Daniel is not an example for us to follow but a pointer to Jesus, the true and greater Daniel! As our Savior, Jesus came into our world of exile, where he lived for us and died for us on the cross. The gospel humbles us when we are smug in our own obedience, reminding us that we are saved by sheer grace alone. The gospel deeply comforts us, reminding us that we stand forgiven and accepted, no matter how much we have failed to live a life of trusting in God's Word and living with integrity.

DISCUSSION *10 MINUTES*

What are some of the messages your culture gives you about identity?

In what ways do you live in the tension between living to please God and the temptation to compromise, blend in, people-please, or protect yourself?

Lesson

1

EXERCISE

GOSPEL IDENTITY—WHO YOU ARE IN CHRIST

20 MINUTES

In our culture today, there is pressure to create your own identity—and it's a fragile one. You have to keep it up to prove yourself, to perform, and to defend yourself. Some people charge ahead with a "fake it till you make it" mentality. Others live in fear of being found out, seen as a phony. Many of us are very sensitive to criticism, which can feel like it's attacking our core being. All of this comes from striving to define ourselves, to create our own identity.

What the gospel offers us is good news indeed. In Christ we *receive* a new identity. You and I are loved as children of God in Christ, now and forevermore! The Christian identity is rooted in grace. You are not saved by what you do (your performance) but by the sheer grace of God in Jesus Christ!

This exercise looks at how we get our identity: building it through the flesh versus receiving it by faith. You'll work on your own as you read a passage of Scripture, answer questions, and write out a prayer.

Then you'll gather with your group to talk about what you noticed as you did this exercise.

Read **Philippians 3:4–11** and respond to the questions in the chart below.

Building identity through the flesh	**Receiving identity in Christ through faith**
Before meeting Christ, what did Paul use to build his identity? See verses 5–6.	When Paul gives up his flesh-built identity, what does he gain? See verses 8–11.
In what ways do you use similar things to build your own sense of identity?	What is most beautiful or compelling to you about the identity we receive through Christ?
One of the ways we might hear ourselves building our identity through the flesh is when we say or think, "At least I . . ." to justify ourselves. Consider what you might say: At least . . . • I am __________ • I have __________ • I do/did __________	Is there an area of flesh-based identity you want to let go of in order to more fully live your identity in Christ? What do you need to remember about the gospel to do that?

Write out a prayer asking God to help you let go of building your identity and instead receive your identity from him.

____

____

____

____

____

____

____

____

____

____

When the group is ready, share some of your responses.

WRAP-UP AND PRAYER *10 MINUTES*

As Christians living in exile, there are cultural forces seeking to shape our identity. It's an act of faith to receive our identity from Christ. And we can't muster up more faith from our own resources—this is the Spirit's work in us! Make praying for this core sense of who we are in Christ part of how you pray for each other throughout this study. Ask God to use this study to equip the members of your group to live by faith in exile, as you await our final homecoming when Jesus returns.

Lesson

2

THE DREAM

BIG IDEA

We may be dismayed by the world's power that can harm us, but we can take heart knowing there is a far greater power that will prevail. Earthly kingdoms come and go, but the Lord will establish his kingdom that will be everlasting.

BIBLE CONVERSATION *20 MINUTES*

A key word in Daniel 2 is *mystery*. A mystery is something that we don't understand, that we don't have the answer to, or that we're troubled by.

As we seek to live by faith in exile, we all experience mystery. We have questions: *What will happen to my life? What's going to happen to my kids? What's going to happen to this world?* There are many things we don't have the answers to, and they can deeply trouble us.

King Nebuchadnezzar has a deeply troubling dream that he doesn't understand; it's a mystery. God reveals the meaning of the dream through Daniel. In this lesson we will look at Nebuchadnezzar's dream and what that means for us today.

Have someone read **Daniel 2** aloud, or have a few readers take turns. Then discuss the questions below:

Nebuchadnezzar's dreams troubled him and he couldn't sleep. What dreams, thoughts, worries, or questions trouble you at night?

In Nebuchadnezzar's search for understanding and meaning, he turns to the magicians and enchanters for help. Who or what do you turn to when you are troubled or need help with a mystery in your life?

We've been talking about how Daniel demonstrates faith as he lives in exile. What does his faith look like and sound like in this chapter?

****

Now read the following article. Take turns reading it aloud, switching readers at each paragraph break. Then discuss the questions that follow the article.

Lesson

ARTICLE

A TROUBLING DREAM, A HOPEFUL FUTURE

5 MINUTES

King Nebuchadnezzar, the most powerful king in all of Babylon, has a dream that troubles him deeply. Some commentaries suggest that he doesn't even remember the contents of the dream because it was so intense and troubling. Distressed by this great mystery, the king turns to the smartest people he knows to interpret his dream, but they are unable to help. In fact, the wisest people in all of Babylon tell the king that the answer he seeks cannot come from mere humans (v. 11)!

There are times when we're trying to find answers to our troubles and life's mysteries, but all the knowledge available in this world comes up short. There must be something more.

When Nebuchadnezzar doesn't get what he wants, he becomes furious and loses his lid (v. 12). His desire to understand his dream becomes a demand. His rage boils over in an evil and ungodly way, and he lashes out at others. Whenever we seek to understand our lives and experiences apart from God, it leads to frustration. Like Nebuchadnezzar, when we are confronted with our inability to make sense of our world and control our lives, we often lash out in anger.

SEEKING GOD WHEN YOU ARE UNCERTAIN

Daniel models another path through our troubles and confusion: He goes to God. In verse 18, Daniel summons his friends to call out to God for mercy, so that he and many others will be saved from the king's wrath.

When the Lord reveals to Daniel the meaning of the king's dream, Daniel blesses God and reflects on his unchanging character (vv. 20–23). Daniel's prayer in this section encourages us to reflect on God's character when we are confronted with difficult situations or danger. God is the God of wisdom. He reveals all things. He knows all things, in darkness and in the light. He has the power to change circumstances and people. And because of this, Daniel is able to trust God and give him praise.

A SOBERING DREAM FOR BABYLON'S KING BUT A HOPEFUL DREAM FOR US!

The image in the dream is a statue made of mixed materials: Its head is gold, its chest and arms are silver, its middle and thighs are bronze, its legs are iron, and its feet are iron mixed with clay. A stone strikes the feet, and the entire statue is broken into pieces and carried away by the wind. But that stone becomes a mountain and fills the whole earth.

The message of the dream is this: Kingdoms come and go. Nebuchadnezzar was thinking, *I'm on top of the world!* And this dream is saying, "Don't you dare think that you've arrived and that you're going to last forever." Kingdoms are always changing. In fact, sin will always cause a lot of disruption, pain, and chaos. But God's kingdom is coming, and it will prevail forever.

JESUS IS THE ROCK

Throughout history, there have been numerous earthly kingdoms. Sadly, many have used their power to crush others with violence and evil. In contrast to the kingdoms of this world, which are both flawed and fleeting, the kingdom that Jesus came to establish is perfect and everlasting.[1]

As the great and powerful King, Jesus is the stone that Daniel 2 speaks of, the One who makes all evil kingdoms crumble and fall. He accomplishes this in the most subversive way. In Colossians 2:15, the apostle Paul writes this about Jesus and his death on the cross: "He disarmed the rulers and authorities and put them to open shame, by triumphing over them in him." On the cross, Jesus dies so as to defeat death, and three days later, he rises from the dead, triumphing in victory as the risen King of kings and Lord of lords!

One day, the King will return and establish his kingdom forever. And on that day, the Lord will wipe every tear from the eyes of those who have suffered yet put their hope in the true King; there will be no more death or mourning or crying or pain, for all "the former things"—including earthly kingdoms of iron, clay, bronze, silver, and gold—will pass away (Revelation 21:4).

This reality is what enables God's people to live as faithful exiles in Babylon. Knowing that Jesus is the powerful King who has established a kingdom that will last forever, we can live with deep hope and resilience, even amid suffering and hardship.

---

1. Mark 1:15

DISCUSSION *10 MINUTES*

Describe a time when you have turned to God for wisdom and understanding.

How does the message of Nebuchadnezzar's dream—that earthly kingdoms are temporary, but God's kingdom is coming and it will prevail—strengthen you to live by faith in exile?

Lesson

EXERCISE

TAKING OUR TROUBLES TO GOD

20 MINUTES

This exercise is an opportunity to better understand your troubles and what they mean beneath the surface. Then you'll consider where you go for help and remember who God is in the midst of your troubles. Work through the following questions on your own and be prepared to share some of your answers with the group.

What troubles weigh on your heart and mind? Like Nebuchadnezzar, we all have things that trouble us. Make a list of some of your troubles in the space provided.

What do your troubles reveal about your deepest needs? Trouble and struggles can often reveal buried areas of unbelief in our hearts. But like Nebuchadnezzar, we need an "interpreter" to help us understand what our struggles reveal about us. Ask the Holy Spirit to show you where you are longing for something other than Christ in the midst of your trouble. Circle any of these words that resonate with you.

My current troubles reveal my desire for __________ apart from Christ:

- Identity
- Meaning
- Purpose
- Success
- Approval
- Security
- Comfort
- Relational harmony
- Belonging

How does the gospel message give you hope and comfort in your troubles? Nebuchadnezzar's dream pointed forward to the kingdom of God. We too live by faith as we wait for God's kingdom to fully arrive. Consider how the good news about Jesus and his coming kingdom speaks into your troubles. Answer one or two of the following questions, naming specific ways that the gospel offers you hope and comfort.

- When I'm longing for identity, meaning, or purpose in the midst of my troubles, how does God provide these things for me? (See Ephesians 1:3–10 for some ideas.)
- When I am chasing after worldly success or approval, what does God offer me that is better? (See Ephesians 1:11–14 for some ideas.)

- When my troubles cause me to chase security or comfort, how does God provide them for me? (See Ephesians 2:4–8 or 2:10 for some ideas.)
- When I feel overwhelmed and want a deep sense of relational harmony and belonging, how does God give me these things? (See Ephesians 2:19–22 for some ideas.)

In your own words, how does the gospel give hope and comfort to you in your troubles?

____

____

____

____

____

When the group is ready, discuss what you learned by doing this exercise.

WRAP-UP AND PRAYER *10 MINUTES*

In your group prayer time, lift up any of the specific troubles that were discussed. Ask God to make the good news of his coming kingdom brighter, clearer, and more real to you. And pray that he would strengthen your faith as you live as exiles.

Lesson

3

THE FIERY FURNACE

BIG IDEA

God's people are called to live with biblical conviction over worldly compromise, even if it entails suffering and persecution for their faith.

BIBLE CONVERSATION *20 MINUTES*

In Daniel 3 we come to the story of the fiery furnace. Here Daniel's three friends—Shadrach, Meshach, and Abednego—have their faith severely tested. King Nebuchadnezzar builds a giant golden statue and calls everyone to worship it—under the threat of death. But these three friends refuse to do so. As a result, they're thrown into the fiery furnace, but God delivers them.

What caused them to do such a brave thing? What was it that so gripped their convictions that led them to respond in such a way, even under persecution and death? How does their story point to Jesus and strengthen our faith today, as we live as exiles in today's "Babylon"?

Now, have someone read **Daniel chapter 3** aloud, or have a few readers take turns. Then discuss the questions below:

If you were in Babylon when King Nebuchadnezzar built the golden statue and issued the decree to worship it, what factors would you weigh in considering your response? How would you approach this situation?

In verses 15–18, what are the three friends sure of, and what is unclear to them? What do they know about God and what do they not know? How does it feel to live in this tension?

What amazes you about the outcome of the fiery furnace (vv. 24–30)?

****

Now read the following article. Take turns reading it aloud, switching readers at each paragraph break. Then discuss the questions that follow the article.

Lesson

FACING THE FIRE

5 MINUTES

At times, the values and beliefs of God's people living in exile will clash with the values and beliefs of the world. In Daniel 3, we see at least four kinds of pressure to conform, compromise, and submit to the Babylonian powers.

1. **Blatant and Unavoidable Pressure (vv. 1–6).** King Nebuchadnezzar builds a gigantic golden image on the plains for all to see. His command for all to fall down and worship the image upon hearing the sound of the trumpet demands a response from people that is public and unavoidable.
2. **Herd Mentality (vv. 3, 7).** A herd mentality is created when everyone is doing something, and it becomes normalized. Here we see "people of influence" worshipping the golden statue. If the "influencers" are doing it, the masses will typically follow.
3. **Harmful Intent (vv. 8–12).** A group of Chaldeans maliciously accuses the Jews of not worshipping the statue. They sink their teeth into Daniel's friends, intentionally playing to the king's pride. They essentially challenge him, "Are you going to let them disrespect you like that?"

4. **Personal Pressure from Authority (vv. 13–15).** It seems as if Nebuchadnezzar views Shadrach, Meshach, and Abednego positively, even wanting to give them a second chance. But his words carry a threat: "If you don't conform, there will be direct consequences."

This story is told in a way that challenges us today. When you're living in exile, there will be pressure to conform to the world and show allegiance to Babylon instead of God. We often view Shadrach, Meshach, and Abednego as heroes of the faith. But the call to live by faith here in Babylon isn't just for "elite" Christians—it's the call for all God's people living in exile. Do you ever feel the pressure from the world? If you're not experiencing any pushback from the world today, you might ask yourself, *Am I compromising? Am I holding fast to the commandment to worship the Lord and him only?*

LIVING BY FAITH

Living by faith can be hard. It can even be fearful. The pressures that come our way may be difficult, and the consequences can be painful, even life-threatening. A closer look at this chapter reveals how we can be comforted in the midst of such challenges.

The writer of Daniel reassures us of God's active presence and saving power even in the way he tells the story. He employs sarcasm to show that what is taking place is a farce. For example, the phrase "set up," which is repeated nine times, communicates that the whole situation is a "set-up" job.[1] The idol itself has to be "set up." It has no inherent power of its own. Like a glance behind the curtain in *The Wizard of Oz*, the language reveals that there's nothing substantial behind the facade of power. Knowing this doesn't take away all the trembling, but humor like this can help one stand against the pressure. As Dale

1. Dale Davis, *The Message of Daniel* (IVP, 2013), 53.

Davis says, “Holy laughter helps you to endure, especially if you see the real weakness behind the veneer of power.”[2]

What does living by faith look like when facing great pressure and persecution from the world?

Living by faith means showing biblical conviction. Bowing to the king’s statue is not something Daniel’s friends even consider (v. 16). Because they are held firm by God’s promises, and because they are rooted in the identity given to them by God, they seek to obey God and fear him more than they fear the king.

Living by faith also means recognizing God’s power that is readily available. Daniel’s friends tell the king, “Our God whom we serve is able to deliver us from the burning fiery furnace” (v. 17). They acknowledge God’s power to save but also recognize that they cannot control or manipulate his power (v. 18). So when we face the fire, we can and should pray for deliverance, trusting that God can deliver us. But God is not a genie in a bottle who grants our every wish. We are to trust in God and put our hope in him, regardless of the outcome. This story highlights obedience—walking by faith—over the outcome.

YOU ARE NOT ALONE IN THE FIRE

For Shadrach, Meshach, and Abednego, obeying God rather than the king has consequences. God doesn’t prevent them from being thrown into the fire. But he brings them through the fire. Perhaps some of you are in the fire today. Maybe you have been there for a long time and you’re questioning why God hasn’t yet delivered you. Our passage reminds us that when we are suffering, we don’t have to be paralyzed by fear because the God who brings you through the fire is also *with* you in the fire.

2. Davis, 54.

When the king looks in the furnace, he says, "I see four men unbound, walking in the midst of the fire, and they are not hurt; and the appearance of the fourth is like a son of the gods" (v. 25). Who is this fourth person in the fire with Shadrach, Meshach, and Abednego? Nebuchadnezzar thinks it is an angel, but in fact it is someone greater.

Centuries after this incident, Jesus would come into this world, voluntarily leaving the comfort and splendor of heaven, precisely so that he could walk through the fire on our behalf and deliver us safely.

On the cross, Jesus experienced two kinds of fire. He willingly endured the fire of persecution from his enemies when they slandered, mocked, tortured, and killed him. But he also experienced the fire of God's wrath when he paid for our sins on the cross. Here in Daniel 3 we see a glimpse of Christ in the physical fire of Nebuchadnezzar's furnace, but in the New Testament the full story of God's love and grace is made clear. We see Jesus, God's own Son, staying in the fire of his Father's judgment, being completely consumed by it, for our sake and out of his great love for us. God has promised to never leave us or forsake us; Jesus kept that promise, even to the point of giving up his own life. And he keeps that promise still.

Knowing all this changes the way we think about our trials and sufferings today. Because Jesus suffered out of great love for us, by faith in the gospel we can suffer out of great love for him. The way to walk through the fire and be free in the midst of it is to focus on the One who not only delivered us from the ultimate fire but is also with us in all our fiery trials today.

DISCUSSION *10 MINUTES*

Of the four kinds of pressures to conform, which is the most similar to what you have experienced?

Which do you think causes faith to grow more: knowing the presence of God with you in a fiery trial or experiencing his deliverance from the trial? Why?

How have you experienced God's presence with you in a "fiery trial" or his deliverance from an impossible situation?

Lesson

FACING THE PRESSURES OF BABYLON

20 MINUTES

In this lesson, we saw four kinds of pressure to conform to the surrounding culture. In this exercise, we are going to consider how we face these pressures in our own lives and how the gospel encourages us in them. Work through the activities below on your own, and then be prepared to share with the group some of what you found.

Fill in the chart below. You can think through any aspect of your life: work or school, home, family, friends, church, or something else. Also consider the cultural messages you consume through media.

Type of Pressure	Example of How I Face This in My Life
Blatant and Unavoidable Pressure	

Type of Pressure	Example of How I Face This in My Life
Herd Mentality	
Harmful Intent	
Personal Pressure from Authority	

Next, choose one of the examples you gave above to consider further.

1. What is this pressure asking me to do? What would it look like to conform to Babylon in this area?

2. In what ways is this pressure asking me to disobey God or to turn away from him?

3. What is on the line if I don't give in to this pressure? What are my fears? What would be "the fiery furnace" if I don't give in?

Finally, consider how the gospel encourages you as you face this pressure.

1. Jesus faced pressures for our sake in his life and ministry, and in his suffering and death. How has Jesus gone through the kind of pressure you are experiencing? (See, for example, Mark 1:12–13 and Matthew 27:39–43.) How does remembering that strengthen you?

2. In addition, Jesus is with you as you face this pressure (Hebrews 13:5–6). He is with you in the fire. What comfort or encouragement do you draw from his presence?

3. What one thing about the gospel do you want to know more fully or have in the front of your mind as you face this pressure?

When the group is ready, have everyone share the one thing they want to know more fully or remember more clearly as they face their pressures.

WRAP-UP AND PRAYER *10 MINUTES*

Pray for one another, asking God's Spirit to impress the truths you discussed on your hearts, to strengthen and encourage you as you live by faith.

Lesson

4

THE HUMBLED KING

BIG IDEA

When pride takes over our lives, we lose our sense of sanity and self. But when we humbly acknowledge God as Lord and King, we can be healed and restored.

BIBLE CONVERSATION *20 MINUTES*

As we study Daniel chapter 4, we're going to look at King Nebuchadnezzar, who was one of the most powerful rulers in the ancient Near East. Because of the prideful way Nebuchadnezzar exalts himself and his unwillingness to properly acknowledge God and his authority, God humbles him by turning him into a wild animal. He begins to eat grass like oxen, and he grows long hair and nails like an eagle. When God graciously restores him, Nebuchadnezzar comes to his senses and praises God. It's a fascinating yet bizarre account.

One of the key questions in Daniel 4 is this: Who reigns and is in control? God reigns! God rules! Humility is acknowledging this reality. The overarching theme of chapter 4 is this statement, which is repeated three times: "The Most High rules the kingdom of men and gives it to whom he will and sets over it the lowliest of men" (vv. 17, 25, 32).

For all of us who live in exile, human pride (the spirit of Babylon) is a constant threat, both from without and from within. Outwardly, there are individuals, people groups, and nations that are oppressive. Inwardly, we wrestle with our own pride that can harm both us and others. In our study, we'll consider our own pride as we look at how God humbled and then restored Nebuchadnezzar.

Have someone read **Daniel chapter 4** aloud, or have a few readers take turns. Then discuss the questions below:

What do you think is the real problem with pride?

Describe a time you became aware of your own pride. Is there a way you were also humbled and restored?

****

Now read the following article. Take turns reading it aloud, switching readers at each paragraph break. Then discuss the questions that follow the article.

Lesson

ARTICLE

PRIDE, HUMILITY, AND HEALING

5 MINUTES

In chapter 4, Nebuchadnezzar writes in first person as if he's giving a testimony. This personal narrative is stunning, given the deep humiliation he experiences. But he has come to realize that there was something poisonous about his pride. And now he's sharing his story with us and praising God for humbling him. As we look at his story, we'll consider human pride and how we can be healed from it.

THE WARNING AGAINST PRIDE (vv. 4–27)

God, in his mercy, warns King Nebuchadnezzar of the danger of pride. He gives the king a dream, and he sends Daniel to interpret the dream, warning Nebuchadnezzar against his pride. With Daniel as a messenger and interpreter of dreams, the Lord essentially says to the king, "Your pride has led to the sins of unrighteousness and the oppression of others" (see v. 27). God mercifully gives Nebuchadnezzar this warning as an opportunity to respond and turn from his prideful ways.

This story also offers readers an opportunity for self-reflection: What warning might God be giving you today against the sin of pride?

THE ATTITUDE BEHIND PRIDE (vv. 28–30)

Pride is marked by a preoccupation with self. King Nebuchadnezzar was one of the most powerful kings in history. In verse 30, he looks at his empire and declares, "Is not this great Babylon, which I have built by my mighty power as a royal residence and for the glory of my majesty?" Nebuchadnezzar takes credit for all that he has and for all that he has accomplished. This is what pride does, and it is a temptation for all of us. This passage invites us to consider how we might be tempted to say in our hearts, "Is not this the great (fill in the blank)?"

It's easy to see how pride can show up when you're experiencing success. But you can also be proud when things are not going well if you are self-focused or self-oriented. Since pride is preoccupation with self, it manifests not only in our successes ("I am great"), but also in our failures ("I am not great"), in our snubs ("You are not great"), and in our fears ("What if I am not great?"). In all of these instances, you are preoccupied with yourself—that's the attitude behind pride.

WHERE PRIDE LEADS (vv. 31–33)

When you come to verses 31–33, you may be thinking, *How bizarre! How strange!* Why did God respond to Nebuchadnezzar's pride by allowing him to become like a wild animal? God could have done many different things to show Nebuchadnezzar his pride. But what a powerful, vivid teaching lesson he chose! When you and I aspire to become greater than other humans and become like God, we actually become less than human, like a wild animal. Nebuchadnezzar's transformation gives us a picture of what happens inside us when pride takes over. God loves us too much to allow us to continue living in pride. So he may bring about a severe mercy to humble you. You may experience humiliation, but God does it not to punish you, but to protect you.

PRIDE: HOW CAN WE BE HEALED? (vv. 34–37)

God graciously shows us where true power lies and what it looks like—and how we can be healed of our foolish pride.

1. Lift up your eyes to God and acknowledge his power (v. 34). When Nebuchadnezzar turned his eyes away from himself and lifted them to God, it was a posture of humility before the One who holds all power. It was an acknowledgment of his need for help and mercy. Notice that Nebuchadnezzar didn't lift up his eyes and make promises that he would be better if only God would heal him. Neither did he lift up his eyes and start pursuing a program of moral reformation. When you and I lift our eyes to God and acknowledge our need for his mercy, we begin to experience "gospel sanity" and receive healing from our pride. The result is humble thanksgiving and praise to the Lord for *his* greatness and mercy.

2. Let the true humble King heal you and restore you. In our passage, we read about King Nebuchadnezzar who was full of pride and was humbled because he thought he was great. In Jesus we see a very different King. Jesus is great because he is humble.

In Philippians 2:5–11, the apostle Paul writes the following about Jesus:

> Have this mind among yourselves, which is yours in Christ Jesus, who, though he was in the form of God, did not count equality with God a thing to be grasped, but emptied himself, by taking the form of a servant, being born in the likeness of men. And being found in human form, he humbled himself by becoming obedient to the point of death, even death on a cross. Therefore God has highly exalted him and bestowed on him the name that is above every name, so that at the name of Jesus every

> knee should bow, in heaven and on earth and under the earth, and every tongue confess that Jesus Christ is Lord, to the glory of God the Father.

What a tremendous difference between these two kings! Nebuchadnezzar was humiliated for *his* sin. King Jesus was humiliated for *our* sin. Jesus's love for us is so great that he was willing to take our sin upon himself and suffer the humiliation we rightly deserved. Our pride, like Nebuchadnezzar's, is egregious, but in God's kindness, Jesus gave up his life so that we could be forgiven and set free from it. When we consider that Jesus chose to suffer for our sake, his humiliation on the cross should both convict us and amaze us. This wonderful truth should convict us and cause us to lift our eyes to God to receive his mercy. At the same time, it should amaze us because Jesus held nothing back in pursuit of us. Such good news should lead us to give thanks and praise to God for his greatness and mercy.

DISCUSSION *10 MINUTES*

What are some similarities between a proud person and a wild animal?

When God humbled Nebuchadnezzar, it made the king look bad. Nevertheless, Nebuchadnezzar gives testimony to what God has done for him. Do you readily share with others when God humbles or corrects you? Why or why not?

Lesson

EXERCISE

SEEKING HEALING FOR OUR PRIDE

20 MINUTES

Let the directions below guide you as you both acknowledge the ways you struggle with pride and look to the One who heals our pride.

PART 1: Being honest about our pride. Pride can take different forms, but we all struggle with it. Sometimes it is subtle, so that it is hard for us to recognize it in ourselves. Ask the Spirit, who searches our hearts, to shine a light on your pride. Remember—when he shows us our pride, it is to heal us, not to harm us.

Pride emerges . . .	Pride sounds like . . .	Ways I see this kind of pride in my own heart
In our successes	"I am great"	

Pride emerges . . .	**Pride sounds like . . .**	**Ways I see this kind of pride in my own heart**
In our failures	"I am not great"	
In our snubs	"You are not great"	
In our fears	"What if I am not great?"	

In what other ways are you preoccupied with yourself?

Pray individually and confess your pride, knowing that Jesus humbled himself to pay the cost for your pride on the cross.

PART 2: Lifting our eyes to God. The solution to pride is not to fix ourselves! It's to look up at God. Shift your gaze to him and let your heart be moved to praise.

Choose one of the following Scripture passages to read and consider God's greatness:

- Daniel 4:34–35
- Philippians 2:5–11
- Colossians 1:15–20

Now write out a prayer of praise to our great God.

WRAP-UP AND PRAYER *10 MINUTES*

Your group might choose to kneel or to lift up your eyes as you pray; these are both postures of humility that would be appropriate in light of Daniel 4. Together, ask for healing for your pride, and praise our great God.

Lesson

5

THE WRITING ON THE WALL

BIG IDEA

For many, the goal of life is to have affluence and influence. Instead of falling for this lie, we must recognize that only God can satisfy us and give our lives meaning.

BIBLE CONVERSATION *20 MINUTES*

The book of Daniel is structured to emphasize three themes about life in exile:

1. Promise (chapters 2 and 7)
2. Persecution (chapters 3 and 6)
3. Pride (chapters 4 and 5)

Promise (chapters 2 and 7). These chapters focus on dreams that reveal the future. We see God and his kingdom prevailing over a world full of heaviness, brokenness, and death. Because Jesus is going to return, and he is our hope, we don't need to lose heart.

Persecution (chapters 3 and 6). These chapters are the accounts of the fiery furnace and the lion's den. Here we see those who are living by faith in exile coming into conflict with the powers of Babylon. But God's people can endure through suffering and live in hope because Jesus, the greater Daniel, suffered on the cross to put an end to all suffering, and one day he will make all things new.

Pride (chapters 4 and 5). Pride is the spirit of Babylon, the world in which we find ourselves. For all of us living in exile, human pride is a constant threat. We are prone to think that the world revolves around us; we believe the lie that God is there to serve us and meet our needs. The poison of pride is that it draws our attention and trust away from God and toward ourselves or other created things.

In the last chapter, we read about the pride of King Nebuchadnezzar. In this chapter, we'll read about King Belshazzar, Nebuchadnezzar's son, who is the last king in Babylon. Belshazzar throws a wild party and brazenly calls for the worship items from God's temple to be brought in and used for his own pleasure. As a result of the king's defiance toward God, a hand appears—the hand of God. The hand writes on the wall, and Belshazzar is terrified. By the end of the night, Belshazzar is dead, and Babylon is overthrown.

Now, have someone read **Daniel chapter 5** aloud, or have a few readers take turns. Then discuss the questions below:

Set the scene of the king's party. If you were filming a video of this chapter, what would your camera show?

King Belshazzar offers a lavish reward to the enchanters (v. 7) and Daniel (v. 16). How do you think the promise of reward could influence those who speak to powerful authorities, for better or for worse?

They say that "the apple doesn't fall far from the tree." In your opinion, is Belshazzar the same as, or different from, his father Nebuchadnezzar?

****

Now read the following article. Take turns reading it aloud, switching readers at each paragraph break. Then discuss the questions at the end of the article.

Lesson

ARTICLE

THE PRIDE OF DEFIANCE TOWARD GOD

5 MINUTES

Pride comes in many forms. Daniel 4 and 5 are both about pride but with a different emphasis. As we have seen, Daniel 4 focuses on the pride of self-promotion and personal greatness. King Nebuchadnezzar looks at his kingdom and boasts, "Is not this great Babylon, which I have built by my mighty power as a royal residence for the glory of my majesty?" (Daniel 4:30).

Daniel 5 focuses on the pride of defiance toward God. King Belshazzar throws a lavish party for a thousand of the most important people in Babylon. To add to his guests' enjoyment, he brazenly calls for the sacred objects that his father had taken from the Lord's temple in Jerusalem. Using the golden vessels from the temple, "they drank wine and praised the gods of gold and silver, bronze, iron, wood, and stone" (Daniel 5:4).

THE CHARACTERISTICS OF PRIDE THAT DEFIES GOD (vv. 1–4)

The pride that defies God is characterized by an attitude of disrespect and dismissiveness toward him. Imagine a person living with a roommate who had a fancy sports car that he cared for meticulously. One day the roommate leaves his keys to the car, and this person decides to take it for a joyride—not just all over town but through the bumpy dirt roads of the mountains. This would be a disrespectful way to treat such a nice car. But more importantly, what the person is doing is very disrespectful toward the roommate who owned the car. This is essentially how King Belshazzar treats the golden vessels that were used for worship in the Lord's temple. He defies God by using the vessels for his own merriment, making a mockery of God by even using them to praise other gods.

Such pride is incredibly foolish. Daniel 5 opens with King Belshazzar throwing a great party, but it ends with his death and the end of his kingdom. Historically, this feast took place while Babylon was under siege by the Medo-Persians. Apparently, that did not matter to Belshazzar. His pride had blinded him to the precariousness of his situation. As Belshazzar feasts and drinks at his party, dismissing God and disrespecting the temple vessels, he assumes nothing will change. But on that very night, his life is taken from him. God delivers him to his enemies because of his foolishness and pride.

GOD'S RESPONSE TO PRIDE THAT DEFIES HIM (vv. 5–28)

In response to Belshazzar's defiance, God supernaturally intervenes with a mysterious hand that writes a cryptic message on the wall. Belshazzar is terrified and desperately tries to understand what it means. As in the past, Daniel is brought in to interpret God's message to the king.

Daniel first tells the king why the writing has appeared, and then he explains what it means. Daniel reminds the king that God made his father, Nebuchadnezzar, powerful and gave him a vast kingdom (v. 18). Seeing how God both humbled and delivered his father should have brought great humility to Belshazzar. However, Daniel points out that "you his son, Belshazzar, have not humbled your heart, though you knew all this" (v. 22). The writing on the wall is a reminder to the king and his court that God's power is far greater than theirs.

After explaining why the writing has appeared, Daniel now explains its message. He states that because of Belshazzar's defiance toward God, the days of his kingdom are numbered. The king has been weighed by the just scales of God's righteousness and has been found guilty. His kingdom will be divided, and the powerful rule of Babylon will be no more.

Belshazzar knew what had happened to his father. He knew about the greatness and power of God. His problem was not one of ignorance but of insolent defiance, and in the end it was his downfall.

THE TRAGIC OUTCOME THAT DOESN'T HAVE TO BE OURS (vv. 29–31)

While we are not specifically told how Belshazzar responded to the Lord upon hearing such news from Daniel, readers cannot help but notice the difference between the ending of chapter 4 and the ending of chapter 5.

At the end of chapter 4, Nebuchadnezzar, healed from his pride, acknowledges God and gives him praise. But with Belshazzar, such praise and humble acknowledgment of God are glaringly absent. Instead, we are told, "That very night, Belshazzar the Chaldean king was killed. And Darius the Mede received the kingdom" (vv. 30–31).

God's judgment of Belshazzar ought to sober us and cause us to examine our own hearts. The Bible tells us that, just like Belshazzar, we stand condemned before God. The writing is on the wall. Romans 3:23 says that "all have sinned and fall short of the glory of God," and Romans 6:23 tells us that "the wages of sin is death." Because of our sin—including our prideful defiance toward God—we have all been found guilty, and our days are numbered. Like Belshazzar, we all have judgment coming our way.

But there is hope and good news! Because of the cross, instead of God's hand of judgment, we can receive God's hand of forgiveness and grace. Consider Jesus hanging on the cross. His hands are nail-pierced. The nails, scars, and blood demonstrate that there had to be judgment for our sinful pride and defiance toward God. This is sobering and humbling. But it is also astonishing. The handwriting of God's judgment came upon Jesus instead of us. In great love, the Son of God took the punishment for our sin—punishment that should have been ours.

Instead of words of judgment coming from the writing on the wall, you and I are able to receive a far different message: "It is finished" (John 19:30). The good news is that Jesus has taken our judgment for sin, and therefore the hand that God extends to you and me is the hand of grace and forgiveness. Hallelujah!

DISCUSSION *10 MINUTES*

How does the world today encourage the pride of defiance (disobedience, disrespect) toward God?

The problem with Belshazzar was not ignorance but insolence. How is it that some people find themselves, like Belshazzar, knowing *about* God while not being in relationship with him or living according to his ways? Have you experienced this? What—or *who*—can change such a person into someone who loves God and seeks to honor him?

Lesson

EXERCISE

TWO HANDS

20 MINUTES

The article contrasts two hands: the hand of judgment, shown in the writing on the wall, and the nail-pierced hand of Jesus, which extends mercy toward us. In this exercise, we are going to consider what it looks and feels like to live under each of these hands.

On your own, look through the characteristics of living under the hand of judgment versus living under the hand of mercy for each of the words written on Belshazzar's wall: "Numbered" (*Mene*), "Weighed" (*Tekel*), and "Divided" (*Parsin*). Take your time with this, reflecting on your own life as you read through these characteristics. Check the qualities you relate to, and put a star beside your top three.

Aramaic Word/Meaning	Living under the hand of judgment	Living under the hand of mercy
***Mene* means "Numbered"**	☐ I have a high need for control over my time; interruptions to my plans annoy or anger me. ☐ I'm driven to overwork. There is so much to get done, I can't afford to take a break. ☐ I need to prove myself and make a name for myself. I strive to leave a legacy. ☐ I have expectations about what my family should look like (getting married, having children) and am overwhelmed with worry that they won't be met (time is ticking). ☐ I compare myself and my accomplishments to others and their accomplishments. ☐ I have a fear of aging that drives me to increasing efforts to improve my appearance or physical health. ☐ I worry about people I love being taken away from me—because of illness or accidents, or because my children will "leave the nest."	☐ I have a growing longing for Christ's return; I look forward to the new creation. ☐ I'm learning to rejoice in trials because I see the Spirit producing character and endurance in me. ☐ I practice Sabbath and receive God's gift of rest. ☐ I receive each day as a gift, welcoming whatever the Lord might have for me that day. ☐ I trust that God has good works for me to walk in (Ephesians 2:10), which he prepared before he laid the foundations of the world, and I seek his help to do them. ☐ As I follow Jesus, my desire to be great is being transformed into a desire to serve. My desire to accumulate wealth is being transformed into cheerful generosity. My desire to make a name for myself is being transformed so I think of myself less and of God more. ☐ I have a growing heart for those who don't yet know Jesus.

Aramaic Word/Meaning	Living under the hand of judgment	Living under the hand of mercy
***Tekel* means "Weighed"**	☐ I often compare myself with others. I feel better when I come out on top, and worse when I see myself as less than. ☐ I respond to my sin with resolve: *I will do better by . . .* ☐ I respond to my sin with penance: *I will make up for this by . . .* ☐ I'm sensitive to criticism. ☐ I try to hide or cover up my faults. ☐ My speech shows how I justify myself: making excuses, blaming others, downplaying my wrongs.	☐ I have a growing appreciation for what Jesus accomplished on the cross. He took my sins away and gave me his righteousness. ☐ I'm able to admit my weaknesses and failures. I don't have to hide or pretend because I'm justified in Christ. ☐ I respond to my sin with faith: *I receive from Christ . . .* ☐ I respond to my sin with repentance: *I turn from sin by . . .* ☐ I'm becoming more compassionate toward those who struggle, because I do too. ☐ The joy and freedom I'm experiencing in the gospel fuel my love for others.

Aramaic Word/Meaning	Living under the hand of judgment	Living under the hand of mercy
***Parsin* means "Divided"**	☐ My life is divided between the religious and the secular parts. ☐ I act and talk differently depending on who I'm with (I struggle with hypocrisy). ☐ I have secret sins that I feel I must keep hidden. If anyone else knew about them, would they accept me? ☐ I hurt over, or am calloused by, broken relationships. ☐ I hold grudges and keep a record of others' wrongs. Forgiveness is hard for me.	☐ Being made friends with God has brought me into relationships with people I wouldn't have previously imagined befriending! ☐ Having received Jesus's forgiveness, I'm growing in my ability to forgive others. ☐ Being in Christ has given me new "family." The gospel empowers us to love each other. ☐ God's Spirit is moving me toward greater wholeness and integrity in my life. ☐ I embrace my own need for the gospel even while inviting others to believe it.

Share with your group a couple of ways you live under both these hands—the hand of judgment and the hand of mercy.

WRAP-UP AND PRAYER *10 MINUTES*

Bearing in mind what you have learned about the hand of judgment and the hand of mercy, pray for the gospel to take deeper root in your lives.

Lesson

6

THE LION'S DEN

BIG IDEA

God is greater than any human king or kingdom. Because the Lord has the power to shut the mouths of any foe or threat, Christians can boldly proclaim, "If God is for us, who can be against us?" (Romans 8:31).

BIBLE CONVERSATION *20 MINUTES*

Many years have passed in Daniel's life. He was a teen in chapter 1, and now in chapter 6, he is eighty years old. But even at eighty Daniel remains in exile, and he continues to live by faith. Whether you are younger or older, God calls you to live by faith as an exile.

Chapters 3 and 6 of the book of Daniel are perhaps the two best-known stories about persecution and not compromising with Babylon. In chapter 3, when the king tries to force Daniel's friends to worship an idol, in faith they respond, "No, we will not!" As a result, they faced the fiery furnace. In chapter 6, when Daniel is commanded through the king's edict to stop worshipping God, in faith he responds, "No, I won't stop!" As a result of his refusal to turn from God, Daniel faces the lion's den. It's a powerful story of deliverance as God shields and protects him.

You'll remember that in Daniel 1–4, Nebuchadnezzar was king of Babylon. In Daniel 5, his son Belshazzar was the last Babylonian king. Now in Daniel 6, the Medo-Persians are in power. Darius is the king, and Daniel is an official in this new kingdom. When other officials become jealous of Daniel's success, they seek a way to get him in trouble. Knowing that Daniel will never stop worshipping God, these officials urge the king to sign an edict declaring a period of worship only to the king. The punishment for refusal is a gruesome death. According to the Medes and the Persians, once the king signed something, it was ironclad; even the king himself couldn't get out of it.

Have someone read **Daniel chapter 6** aloud, or have a few readers take turns. Then discuss the questions below:

What kinds of pressures does Daniel face in this chapter?

If you were an exile when the king's decree went out, what would you have to work through as you figured out how to respond?

How does Daniel's living by faith impact others in this account?

*****

Next, read this lesson's article. Take turns reading it aloud, switching readers at each paragraph break. Then discuss the questions that follow.

Lesson

ENGAGING—AND NOT ENGAGING—BABYLON

5 MINUTES

GOD'S PEOPLE ARE CALLED TO BOTH ENGAGE AND NOT ENGAGE THE WORLD

As Daniel lives by faith in exile, he engages Babylon (vv. 1–5). He is working in the public sphere, promoting the good of Babylon so that the king might suffer no loss. As exiles, God's people are to promote the good of society and the world. The prophet Jeremiah had instructed the exiles to "seek the welfare of the city where I have sent you into exile, and pray to the Lord on its behalf, for in its welfare you will find your welfare" (Jeremiah 29:7). This is what Daniel does and what we are to do as we live in the world.

But there are limits to our engagement (vv. 6–10). When Daniel hears about King Darius's ordinance prohibiting anyone from making a petition to any god or man except the king, he refuses to comply. He doesn't show off and he doesn't hide—he continues to pray to God with the windows open, just as he had been doing. Living by faith in exile means we must not engage when engagement requires assimilation or compromise.

Living in exile is not easy. Daniel faces conflict both when he serves the king and when he refuses to assimilate or compromise. It is clear the king favors Daniel (v. 14). Yet even the most powerful ruler in all the land can't avoid the conflict between the rule of man and the rule of God. Persecution still comes to Daniel, despite the king's best efforts.

As Christ's followers, we will unavoidably have conflict with the values of this world. Jesus forewarned his followers that they would face persecution.[1] So Christians should not be surprised when there's tension and conflict between the City of God and the City of Man. But God provides hope and strength to help his people both engage and not engage the world.

What is this hope and strength?

God himself. *The living God whom we serve is the ultimate Deliverer.*

BE CAREFUL WHAT YOU TAKE AWAY FROM THIS STORY

This story of Daniel is well known, yet it has often been taught in a way that has been not only unhelpful, but harmful. There's a moralistic teaching that says, "If you are faithful and blameless, God will deliver you out of your 'lion's den.'"

How is this kind of thinking unhelpful and even harmful?

It is easy to fall into the trap of thinking, *If I do ___ for God, he will give me ___*. The problem with this way of relating to God is that it makes his care for us dependent on our performance instead of his grace. It makes us focus on "earning" something from God instead of receiving his mercy through sheer grace: "*I need to* have more faith; *I need to* be more blameless. God's not delivering me, so *I need to* be

1. John 15:19

more like Daniel; *I need to* become more faithful." Thinking this way causes a deep sense of anxiety and angst.

In extreme cases, this type of moralistic approach can even lead us away from God. How? We begin to say to ourselves, "I was faithful like Daniel, but God didn't deliver me from my lion's den. And I know people who loved God, and God didn't deliver them either. In fact, I know plenty of people who don't love God at all and they seem to prosper." When we focus on our performance instead of God's faithfulness, our relationship with God is inevitably harmed.

Moralism is *not* what this chapter is teaching. And it is certainly *not* what Christianity is teaching! How do we know?

There was someone far more faithful, far more blameless, than Daniel: Jesus. In the garden of Gethsemane, Jesus asked if his lion's den, the cup of suffering on the cross, could pass from him. But in order to secure our salvation, God did not rescue him. Jesus experienced the ultimate lion's den as he hung on the cross, suffered, and died for our sins. Though he had no sin, despite his perfect faith, the Father did not spare Jesus from the cross. Christ took on the punishment for our sin, laying down his sinless and perfect life in our stead, so that we can receive the gift of salvation.

SEEING JESUS IN THE LION'S DEN

Looking at the cross, we see that Jesus is the better Daniel. Just as Daniel was wrongfully accused, Jesus was wrongfully accused. Daniel was thrown into the pit and left to die; the next morning, Daniel came out from the pit alive. So too, Jesus, the greater Daniel, was thrown into the pit where he *did* die, and on the third day, on that Easter morning, he came out alive from the pit of death. The difference is that Daniel was saved from death, but Jesus conquered death and was raised from the grave. The living God whom we serve is the great Deliverer!

If you know that Jesus went to the ultimate lion's den for your sake, you will be able to confront the various "lion's dens" in your life. The central lesson of Daniel is that it is the Lord who reigns. Therefore, take heart! Even in exile the living God—Jesus, the risen King—is the ultimate Deliverer. And he is with you. He will never leave you.

DISCUSSION *10 MINUTES*

The article talked about how we are to engage and not engage with the world. What do you think prevents Christian exiles from engaging in Babylon and seeking its welfare? What are some reasons why exiles engage the surrounding culture, even when it conflicts with obeying God?

In Daniel, we keep facing the reality that living by faith in exile will lead to persecution. How is this sitting with you?

How have you seen moralistic teaching be harmful in your life or in the lives of others?

Lesson

EXERCISE

TO ENGAGE OR NOT TO ENGAGE?

20 MINUTES

What will happen when you both engage and do not engage the world? Your life will repel some people and be attractive to others. You see this with Daniel. His colleagues are jealous of him and repelled by his values, so they set a trap to get Daniel punished for praying to God. King Darius, on the other hand, sees how Daniel's faith in his God has led to a life of integrity, and he is attracted to such a beautiful and bold life of faith.

In this exercise you'll work individually through the questions to consider how you engage and don't engage with the Babylon of the world you live in. Then you'll come back together with your group to discuss what you noticed and pray for each other.

As we navigate life in exile, most of us probably lean one way or the other. Our natural tendencies lead us either to engage too much or to not engage where we should.

- How would you describe your own tendency to engage or not engage Babylon? Or in what ways do you see both of these tendencies in yourself?

It's easy to forget that we are called to love others, even when navigating the challenges of living in exile.

- What does it look like for you to seek the welfare of others and the welfare of your city?

- Who is someone that God might be leading you to enter into a deeper relationship with?

- How will taking these actions require faith on your part?

Think of an example from your life that illustrates your struggle to follow God in exile.

- Can you name a time when you didn't live by faith and avoided doing something you *should* have done? What happened as a result?

- Can you name a time when you compromised or assimilated to the culture and did something you *shouldn't* have done? What happened as a result?

- What did you need to remember about God and his promises that would have helped you in each of those moments?

As you think about your answers, remember that Jesus is the ultimate Deliverer. He is with you wherever you go. Because he suffered the greater lion's den of the cross, we stand forgiven, made new, and empowered by the Holy Spirit. Ask for his help to live by faith in Babylon.

When everyone is ready, share with the group a way you need God's help to live by faith in exile.

WRAP-UP AND PRAYER *10 MINUTES*

In your prayer, remember that Jesus went before you to the lion's den when he went to the cross, and he is with you in exile. Pray for each other, that God would increase your faith as you seek the welfare of your Babylon without compromising your love and obedience to the true King.

Lesson

7

THE FOUR BEASTS

BIG IDEA

The world we live in is beastly, but God is sovereign and will ultimately prevail—so have hope!

BIBLE CONVERSATION *20 MINUTES*

There are two parts to the book of Daniel. The first six chapters are essentially the narrative section. That section asks, "What does it look like to live in exile?" The last six chapters are the apocalyptic section. This section looks ahead and asks, "What will happen after exile? Where is all this headed?"

The biblical apocalyptic writings sound strange to our modern ears. We wonder how to understand them. How can we wrap our minds around what we read in the second half of Daniel?

One way to understand the apocalyptic portion of Daniel is to view it as a picture book rather than a puzzle book.[1] If we approach these chapters like a puzzle that needs to be solved, we're likely to miss God's overall intention and purpose. Instead, because apocalyptic

1. Vern S. Poythress, *The Returning King: A Guide to the Book of Revelation* (P&R Publishing, 2000), 13. Although Poythress is referring to the book of Revelation, I am applying the picture book approach to the second half of Daniel.

writing makes frequent use of images, and "images communicate truth . . . but not with precision,"[2] it's better to read these chapters the way we would read a picture book.

Rather than trying to figure out what each piece of the puzzle means, we need to ask, *What is the purpose of these pictures?* The images can be terrifying, but they're not intended to frighten us and paralyze us with fear. As Iain Duguid notes, "The purpose is not to give us nightmares, but to calm our nightmares."[3] Throughout the apocalyptic portion of Daniel, the overarching message is that even though the world can be a terrifying place, God's power is peerless, and he is the victorious Warrior and King. As we consider terrible events that have occurred in history, or as we look at the evil and brokenness in our current world, we would be overcome with fear if we didn't have the assurance that God is the sovereign Lord of all things.

Finally, note the sandwich structure of this chapter. Human conflict is highlighted at the beginning and end, but sandwiched in between is the central theme of God's reign and rule:

1. The world we live in is beastly (vv. 1–8).
2. The Lord is sovereign and will ultimately prevail (vv. 9–14).
3. The beastly nature will continue to rage and will even escalate (vv. 15–28).

Now, have someone read **Daniel chapter 7** aloud, or have a few readers take turns. Then discuss the questions below:

---

2. Tremper Longman, *Daniel*, NIV Application Commentary (Zondervan Academic, 1999), 192.

3. Iain M. Duguid, *Daniel*, Reformed Expository Commentary (P&R Publishing, 2008), 112.

What stands out to you about the images in this chapter?

When Daniel received this vision, he was anxious and alarmed (v. 15). How then do you suppose the purpose of this vision is "to calm our nightmares"?[4]

****

Now read the following article. Take turns reading it aloud, switching readers at each paragraph break. Then discuss the questions that follow the article.

4. Duguid, *Daniel*, 112.

Lesson

ARTICLE

THE BEASTS AND GOD'S TRIUMPH

5 MINUTES

THE FOUR BEASTS: THE WORLD WE LIVE IN IS BEASTLY (vv. 1–8 AND 15–28)

Chapter 7 takes us back in time to the first year of the reign of Belshazzar, the last king of Babylon, and a dream that Daniel had. In his dream, Daniel sees four beasts coming out of the sea of chaos. He describes these creatures as animal-like but distorted, reflecting the distortion of evil and brokenness in our world. There is a predatory lion-eagle that stands upright like a human, a bear that devours flesh, a winged leopard that is given dominion, and a horned creature that is too terrifying to describe.

Later Daniel gives us the interpretation and meaning of these unnatural creatures: "These four great beasts are four kings who shall arise out of the earth. But the saints of the Most High shall receive the kingdom and possess the kingdom forever, forever and ever" (vv. 17–18).

Many biblical scholars suggest that the great beasts describe the nature of all earthly kingdoms in human history. In the New Testament Paul speaks of the time from the fall of humanity until Jesus returns in glory as "the present evil age" (Galatians 1:4). We are living in this present evil age, in which evil human kingdoms are like mutant beasts that seek to devour and destroy.

Furthermore, there is increasing intensity in these images—each animal seems to have greater power and to be a greater threat. The fourth is a beast with ten horns and iron teeth, more terrifying and powerful than the rest. Horns in the Old Testament represented power, like a horned animal that is aggressive. And here, there are ten horns! Note the little horn that's personified (v. 8): the "eyes like the eyes of a man" tell us that it is intelligent, and the "great things" that its mouth speaks are blasphemous words.

It can be tempting to treat this like a puzzle and try to figure out exactly which kingdoms in human history are being described and what the timeline is for how things will unfold. But remember, this is not a puzzle book but a picture book! Its pictures show us that this world that stands against God is terrifying and bestial, and that, given the nature of sin, this beastliness will grow and get worse.

The Bible does not sugarcoat how evil and broken this world can be. Oftentimes, when people find out that I'm a pastor, one of the things they'll say is, "I have a problem with Christianity—there's a lot of talk of sin and judgment." My response in light of this chapter would be, "Because this world is really beast-like!" I was a history major in college; it doesn't matter what culture you look at, whether ancient or modern, there are horrific acts of violence and evil on a scale that is just shocking. The Bible doesn't ignore or minimize this. It speaks honestly about the utter brokenness of the world we live in.

THE LORD IS SOVEREIGN, AND HE WILL ULTIMATELY PREVAIL (vv. 9–14)

As mentioned earlier, this whole chapter has a sandwich structure that focuses our attention on the central fact that the Lord will prevail. As we zoom in and look more carefully at the center of this chapter

(vv. 9–14), we notice that there is a sandwich structure within the sandwich structure. We see three things in this sandwich-within-a-sandwich:

First, we see the Ancient of Days, who judges with power (vv. 9–10). *Ancient of Days* describes God, who is the Alpha and Omega. He lives forever and his reign lasts forever—in contrast to evil kings and kingdoms. While all the earthly kingdoms and beasts are frenetic with activity and anxiety, the Ancient of Days is neither anxious nor frenetic but in complete control—he takes his seat. There, he judges all evil with just fury.

Second, we see the beast defeated (vv. 11–12). In verse 11 the beast is killed. Here, at the climax at the center of the chapter, the enemy is vanquished. But this is no epic battle; this is no raging intense fight. The writer is telling us that although the beast seems terrifying and powerful, really, it's a little horn. It talks a big game, but before God, it's no threat whatsoever. God takes it out; it is utterly destroyed.

Third, we see the Son of Man (vv. 13–14). Then in Daniel's vision "there came one like a son of man." This man is unique; he is unlike all the distorted beasts. He comes from the clouds of heaven, the divine glory and presence of God. To him the Ancient of Days gives all dominion and glory and an everlasting kingdom—meaning he is royalty, the King of kings, victorious with great authority and power.

Friends, the Ancient of Days and the Son of Man point us to Jesus, who triumphs over his enemies through his death on the cross and his resurrection.[5] And one day, there will be the ultimate and complete triumph over evil!

---

5. Colossians 2:14–15

KNOWING GOD WILL TRIUMPH, STAY HOPEFUL

Paul says in Romans 8:31, 37–39:

> What then shall we say to these things? If God is for us, who can be against us? . . . No, in all these things we are more than conquerors through him who loved us. For I am sure that neither death nor life, nor angels nor rulers, nor things present nor things to come, nor powers, nor height nor depth, nor anything else in all creation, will be able to separate us from the love of God in Christ Jesus our Lord.

In light of Daniel 7, we could rephrase what Paul says like this:

> Because of Christ's victory, I am sure that neither beasts, nor any beast-like creatures, nor horns, nor little horns with big mouths—nothing will be able to separate us from the love of God in Christ Jesus, our Lord.

As we study the apocalyptic literature of Daniel, the real goal isn't to simply understand more about Scripture. Of course, it is good and important for us to know the meaning of the Bible. But may our deepest takeaway be worship that proclaims, "Praise God, JESUS WINS!" Since Jesus wins, we can stay hopeful. Because Christ has triumphed, one day we too will triumph in him. That's the real message of Daniel 7.

DISCUSSION *10 MINUTES*

How does Daniel's vision pull back the curtain of worldly power?

In what ways does knowing that God will triumph give us courage to live by faith in exile?

Lesson

7

THE HOPE WE HAVE OF GOD'S TRIUMPH

20 MINUTES

The world we live in is beastly, and we encounter different forms of beasts in our exile. In this exercise, we're going to strengthen our hope as we look at God's triumph.

On your own you will look up several of the Bible verses below. As you read each passage, think through how it speaks of God's triumph over different kinds of struggles. Write down your reflections in the space provided and be ready to share one or two of your insights with the rest of the group.

Over sin

- Colossians 2:13–15

____

____

____

Over sadness

- Revelation 21:1–4

___

___

___

Over death

- 1 Corinthians 15:54–57

___

___

___

Over broken relationships

- Ephesians 2:14–17

___

___

___

Over international conflict and strife

- Isaiah 11:6–9

___

___

___

Over all things

- Ephesians 1:19–23

____

____

____

In what ways does the certainty of God's triumph give you hope now?

____

____

____

____

____

____

____

When your group is ready, discuss how God's triumph encourages you and gives you hope.

WRAP-UP AND PRAYER *10 MINUTES*

When you are ready to pray, spend time praising God for his ultimate victory.

Lesson

8

THE RAM AND THE GOAT

BIG IDEA

Even in the suffering and struggle of living in exile, God is still in control and will ultimately put all things right.

BIBLE CONVERSATION *20 MINUTES*

It has been observed that when Christians are facing persecution for their faith, the two most comforting books in the Bible are Daniel and Revelation. Why is that? Because these books speak to the nightmares they are experiencing and remind them that Jesus wins.

Even those of us who don't experience intense persecution struggle when faced with evil. Whether it's personal suffering or the brokenness we see in the fallen world around us, there is evil everywhere—and as believers, we are not immune from it. The beasts we looked at in the last chapter can cause nightmares.

The placement of chapters 7 and 8 together highlights the contrast between them. Daniel 7 has a wide lens, zooming out to show readers what will happen after the exile. It gives us a whole-world perspective and pulls back the curtain to reveal what is happening on a cosmic level.

Daniel 8 has a narrower lens. This chapter zooms in to Daniel's particular historical context (verse 2, for example, gives specific place names). The vision shows what will happen after Israel's exile. Here, the ram is a reference to the empire of the Medo-Persians (v. 20), and the goat is a reference to Greece (v. 21). As we have seen, horns signify power and pride. The horns in this chapter represent kings and kingdoms within the Medo-Persian and Greek empires.

Now, have someone read **Daniel chapter 8** aloud, or have a few readers take turns. Then discuss the questions below:

How would you describe the imagery used here? What feelings does it evoke?

What questions do you have reading this?

Why do you think Daniel responds to this vision the way he does (v. 27)?

How would this vision have encouraged exiles in Daniel's time to live by faith?

****

Now read the following article. Take turns reading it aloud, switching readers at each paragraph break. Then discuss the questions that follow the article.

Lesson

SUFFERING AND GOD'S SOVEREIGNTY

5 MINUTES

The vision of the ram and the goat in Daniel 8 highlights key themes that we all face while living in exile: suffering, struggle, and God's sovereignty.

IN EXILE, SUFFERING WILL ALWAYS BE A REALITY

There will always be rams and goats and little horns roaming among the nations, speaking defiant words—and God's people will often be in the crossfire. This was true in Daniel's day, and it's true in our day.

The suffering we encounter as a result takes place on multiple levels: personal, geopolitical, and spiritual. As Daniel himself experienced in his capture and exile, suffering is personal. On a geopolitical level, we see the suffering that's caused by nations raging against one another. Suffering can also be spiritual, taking the form of an attack against God and his people.

Suffering reminds us that sin, exile, and judgment are realities everyone must face. It can be tempting for us as Christians to think, *Since we're the good people and those are the bad people, we should be exempt from suffering.* Daniel's writings remind us that instead of thinking in terms of "good" versus "bad" people, we should think in terms of proud versus humble people. Humble people realize there aren't any good people, so everyone needs Jesus for salvation!

In the Bible, the theme of exile begins well before the events described in the book of Daniel. At the beginning, in Genesis, Adam and Eve live in the garden. But when they first sin, they are banished from it. In other words, they are sent into exile. This exile is then replayed later in the Old Testament. God's people repeatedly worship idols and reject God. The prophets repeatedly call upon God's people to repent, but they do not. So what happens? Eventually, they are sent into exile because of their sin.

Adam and Eve's story is our story. Israel's story is our story too. This is humbling. Remember, all of us were banished from God's presence because of our sin. But Jesus is the One who brings us home. Don't make the mistake of thinking, *We're the good people, so we deserve to be treated differently from the bad people.* None of us are "good" by God's standards. Rather, we are to be humble people who realize we need Jesus to save us from our sin by taking our judgment upon himself, so that he can bring us home from exile.

IF SUFFERING IS A REALITY, HOW DO WE LIVE BY FAITH IN EXILE?

Living by faith in exile won't happen by relying on our own strength and power. The goal is not to hunker down and bear our suffering through our own abilities, strength, and resources. Instead, we endure suffering faithfully by depending on God and his work in us.

Consider Paul's prayers for the saints who are suffering in Ephesians 3:14–19:[1]

---

1. See Acts 19:23–31 for an account of persecution in Ephesus.

> For this reason I bow my knees before the Father, from whom every family in heaven and on earth is named, that according to the riches of his glory *he may grant you to be strengthened with power through his Spirit in your inner being,* so that Christ may dwell in your hearts through faith—that you, being rooted and grounded in love, may have strength to comprehend with all the saints what is the breadth and length and height and depth, and to know the love of Christ that surpasses knowledge, that you may be filled with all the fullness of God. (emphasis added)

When Paul prays for Christians who are suffering because of their faith, he does not pray, "Curse the evil people harming us! Get rid of them!" Rather, he prays that the gospel would go deeper in their lives; he prays that they would know and experience the love of God for them in Christ. Why? Because when we experience the love and power of the gospel going deeper into our hearts, we will be resilient and strengthened through his Spirit in our inner being. God will keep us through our suffering and sustain us with the beauty and greatness of his love for us.

GOD'S SOVEREIGNTY AND THE END OF SUFFERING

God's sovereignty means that God knows all things and has power over all things. He gave Daniel this vision of the ram and the goat before the events occurred in history. God is not caught off guard; he's not scared. Kingdoms come and go, but God reigns forever.

God tells us what is to come and reminds us that he will defeat all evil, so that we won't be anxious or caught off guard. *In God's sovereignty, suffering has an expiration date.* In his vision, Daniel is told that the terrible events he sees will last "2,300 evenings and mornings" (v. 14). There are various interpretations of the meaning of this phrase, but this much is clear: Suffering is limited and time-bound. It will not last forever.

You may be wondering, "How can I know that suffering will not last forever?" In the gospel, we have a God who understands suffering and has even experienced deep suffering. The cross is the place of our Savior's profound suffering for our sin, but it is also the place of Christ's great victory over sin. When Jesus cried out, "It is finished" (John 19:30), the work of redemption was complete. Jesus suffered to put an end to all suffering!

In 1 Corinthians 15:57, as the apostle Paul reflects on Christ's victory over sin through his death and resurrection, he writes, "But thanks be to God, who gives us the victory through our Lord Jesus Christ."

So if you find yourself struggling and discouraged today, take heart and remember this: The victory is the Lord's. Hear the words of Jesus: "I have said these things to you, that in me you may have peace. In the world you will have tribulation. But take heart; I have overcome the world" (John 16:33).

DISCUSSION *10 MINUTES*

How would you explain the gospel to a friend using the theme of exile?

What are the pitfalls and dangers of trying to endure suffering in our own strength, rather than in dependence on God?

How is the "expiration date" of suffering a hope and encouragement to you?

Lesson

TURN YOUR EYES UPON JESUS

20 MINUTES

As God's people, there are days when we look at suffering that takes place in the world and our faith feels strong: "If God is for us, who can be against us?[2] Jesus is going to win! God is with us!"

Then there are other days when we look at suffering that takes place in the world and our faith feels weak: "Where is the Lord in all of this? How long, O Lord, will we struggle and be overcome with anxiety and fear?"

Even with the deep faith Daniel had in the Lord, he too found himself weak and overwhelmed at times. At the end of Daniel 8, Daniel is overcome and unable to get out of bed, appalled by the visions he has had (v. 27).

When you feel overwhelmed and distraught, consider King Jehoshaphat's prayer. In 2 Chronicles 20:12, when the kingdom of Judah is attacked by two countries, Jehoshaphat prays, "Our God, will you not judge them? For we have no power to face this vast army

2. Romans 8:31

that is attacking us. We do not know what to do, but our eyes are on you" (NIV).

For this exercise, we're going to consider where we struggle to live by faith in exile. Then we are going to practice looking to Jesus, fixing our eyes upon him. Work through the questions below on your own, and when the group is ready, come back together.

NAMING OUR STRUGGLES. In your experience of exile, where are you struggling currently? Jot down a few notes about what the situation is and how you are struggling with it. If you are having a hard time coming up with an answer, think about places where you are struggling to know what to do, are going through suffering, or are anxious about the direction society is going.

____

____

____

____

____

Now, let's look at some of the names of God that reveal who he is. We'll consider how his name encourages and strengthens us while we live in exile.

JEHOVAH NISSI: THE LORD IS MY BANNER

> And Moses built an altar and called the name of it, The LORD Is My Banner. (Exodus 17:15)

Jehovah Nissi signifies God's protection over his people. Moses used this name for God after God gave Israel a miraculous victory over the

Amalekites. This name reminds us that God is the One who fights for us and defends us.

How this name encourages us in exile:

____

____

____

JEHOVAH GIBBOR: THE LORD, THE MIGHTY WARRIOR

> Who is this King of glory? The Lord, strong and mighty,
> the Lord, mighty in battle! (Psalm 24:8)

Jehovah Gibbor is a name that highlights God's power and might in battle. It is used in the context of God fighting on behalf of his people and delivering them from their enemies.

How this name encourages us in exile:

____

____

____

JEHOVAH SABAOTH: THE LORD OF HOSTS/ ARMIES

> God is our refuge and strength, an ever-present help in trouble. Therefore we will not fear, though the earth give way and the mountains fall into the heart of the sea. (Psalm 46:1–2 niv)

> "Be still, and know that I am God. I will be exalted among the nations, I will be exalted in the earth!" The Lord of hosts is with us; the God of Jacob is our fortress. (Psalm 46:10–11)

Jehovah Sabaoth is the name that reflects God's power and authority over all the forces of heaven and earth. This name is used in the context of spiritual warfare, telling us that God is our protector and deliverer in times of trouble.

How this name encourages us in exile:

____

____

____

One final encouragement: Jesus bears all three of these names. He is the Lord our banner, the Lord our warrior, the Lord of hosts, who fights for us, who died on the cross and rose again for us, who triumphs and wins for us! And one day, the Prince of Peace will bring eternal shalom when he returns. This gives us hope even as we live in exile.

How does looking at who God is, directing our eyes to him, help you in your suffering and struggle?

____

____

____

If we're honest, many of us will work through this and still have doubts and questions. That's okay. Remember that when Daniel's friends were to be thrown into the fiery furnace and when Daniel himself was facing the lion's den—they didn't know what the outcome would be. But they looked to the Lord in faith.

Faith is looking to the God who is with you; it is not a guarantee of a certain outcome. Ask God to help you in your uncertainty as you struggle and suffer.

When the group comes back together, discuss your experience of looking to Jesus in your uncertainty. How did God encourage you in this exercise? How are you still struggling?

WRAP-UP AND PRAYER *10 MINUTES*

Your group is a community to hold each other's stories as you live together in exile. There's no need for you to provide solutions or fix each other. Rather, carry each other's needs to the throne of grace in prayer. Take time to do that now.

Lesson

9

THE PRAYER AND SEVENTY WEEKS

BIG IDEA

When we readily repent of our sins and turn to God in prayer, life in exile will be characterized by humility and hope.

BIBLE CONVERSATION *20 MINUTES*

As we begin Daniel 9, it will be helpful to remember why God's people are in exile to begin with: It is a result of their sin. When the Israelites prepared to take the promised land, God laid out blessings for obedience and curses for disobedience.[1] Once they were living in the land, the people sinned and disobeyed God—and God justly punished them by sending them into exile. Yet, as we will see in this chapter, even in exile, God's people have been unrepentant (vv. 12–13).

We will look at the prayer Daniel offers up while in exile, and we will see his heart posture. In response to his prayer, there is a vision—the angel Gabriel appears to tell Daniel what is to come after the Israelites' time of exile (seventy weeks).

1. Deuteronomy 28:36–68

Now, have someone read **Daniel chapter 9** aloud, or have a few readers take turns. Then discuss the questions below:

What Daniel encountered in the Scriptures caused him to pray and make confession. Have you experienced a time when hearing from God's Word led you to confession? If you have, what was that experience like? If you haven't, why do you think that is?

What gives you hope in Gabriel's message to Daniel (vv. 20–27)? What confuses you?

****

Now read the following article. Take turns reading it aloud, switching readers at each paragraph break. Then discuss the questions that follow the article.

Lesson

ARTICLE

HUMBLE AND HOPEFUL

5 MINUTES

As we study Daniel 9, it might be easy to lose sight of the forest on account of all the trees. The big idea we want to come away with has to do with our heart. What should the posture of our heart be as we live in exile? This chapter shows us. In it we see first a **humble** posture of conviction over sin (Daniel's prayer) and second a **hopeful** posture (Gabriel's response to Daniel's prayer).

A HUMBLE POSTURE

Why is it important to have a humble posture of conviction over sin? In the previous lesson, we talked about how easy it is to operate out of the categories of "good" and "bad" people. We are tempted to think, *We are the good people and those over there are the bad people.* But this way of thinking ignores the biblical reality that "none is righteous, no, not one" (Romans 3:10) and "no one is good except God alone" (Mark 10:18).

As we have seen, instead of operating out of a "good versus bad" paradigm, Christians operate out of a "proud versus humble" paradigm.

In our fallen nature, we are all proud, and we all live for ourselves. In contrast, humility recognizes, "I am not good. I need Jesus."

How do you know if you are operating out of a "proud versus humble" paradigm? If you are, you will experience conviction of sin. We see such conviction of sin in the way Daniel reads God's Word and the way he prays.

Engaging God's Word should bring conviction of sin; it should bring about repentance and faith. From the prayer Daniel prays, it is clear that through his study of God's Word (vv. 1–3), he is convicted of sin.

Paradoxically, sometimes our good deeds can get in the way of our ability to see our true need for God's grace and short-circuit conviction of sin. It can be tempting to believe that God's love for us is determined by our obedience, instead of God's mercy. This mentality often leads to either self-righteousness (*Look how much more moral I am than others!*) or despair (*I feel like a fraud! I am constantly failing and will never pass muster!*). We may "beat others up" who we think are not as good and moral as we are, or we may "beat ourselves up" because we think we are not as good and moral as others. Both these responses are forms of pride.

How does a humble heart encounter God's Word? Have you ever stood next to someone and realized that person is more beautiful, more powerful, more successful than you? Being around such a "great" person highlights your imperfections and shortcomings. This happens to a far greater degree when we approach God! As we come before God's beauty and perfection, we see our own sins and shortcomings. We immediately realize that we "fall short of the glory of God" (Romans 3:23).

The conviction of sin Daniel experiences when reading God's Word in turn impacts how he prays. Daniel sees his own sins—notice how he prays "me" and "we." He does not say, "*Lord, forgive them because they have sinned against you. They are rebellious.*" If you find that you are constantly praying like that, then you may be operating out of the "good versus bad" people paradigm. Daniel sees his own sin and admits on his behalf and on behalf of all the Israelites, "We have sinned" (vv. 5, 8, 11, 15).

Christian friends, we are people who sin and desperately need the grace of the gospel. As we read God's Word, our hearts should become more and more humble before the perfect radiance and beauty of our God.

A HOPEFUL POSTURE

The angel Gabriel comes to Daniel in response to his prayer. Before getting into the details of his message, Gabriel reassures Daniel, "You are greatly loved" (v. 23). What an important reminder to Daniel, who has endured decades of exile. And what an important reminder to those of us living in exile today: We are loved! We are loved even when suffering and hardship come our way. We are loved not because of what we have done, but because of God's covenant love. We are loved in Christ.

Having given Daniel reassurance of God's steadfast love, Gabriel now turns to the contents of the message he has come to deliver. This message is admittedly confusing, and scholars have varied interpretations. I don't want us to lose the forest for the trees: Gabriel is giving Daniel a message of hope to help him persevere in exile. It looks past the end of exile to a future that is securely in God's hand.

For those of us on the other side of the cross, Gabriel's message reminds us of our sure hope in Christ. Let's look at this hope by considering three themes that are woven into Gabriel's message: exile, covenant, and Jubilee.

- **Exile:** There is a time that God has set when our exile—like that of the Israelites—will come to an end. Jesus, who was exiled and cast out on the cross, will bring us home from exile.
- **Covenant:** God's covenant of grace is one-sided. Just as the release of the Israelites did not depend on them, so our deliverance does not depend on us. Rather, God says, "*I* promise, *I* will do this."[2] Christ's death and resurrection remind us that all the promises of God are yes and amen.[3] And one day, we who have put our trust in Jesus will come home from exile, not because of our effort, but all because of Jesus.
- **Jubilee:** In Old Testament times, God decreed that the Israelites were to observe a Jubilee year every "seven weeks of years"—that is, every forty-nine years (Leviticus 25:8). It was to be a year of liberty and rest for all the people and the land.[4] The seventy weeks and seven weeks in Gabriel's message call to mind the theme of Jubilee. For all of us who are in Christ, Jesus is our Jubilee, and he sets us free from sin and death. Now what awaits us is the *ultimate* Jubilee, when Jesus will defeat sin, evil, and death once and for all. At the same time, he will usher in the eternal rest, feast, and celebration of our homecoming with him.

Daniel 9 shows us how God's people in exile are both humble and hopeful. Like Daniel, Christians see the brokenness and sin in themselves and in the world, and what we see causes us to grieve and call out to God. Because we recognize the brokenness and sin in our own hearts, we do not simply point fingers and blame others as the problem but acknowledge our own part in the problem. As a result, we have a humble posture before God and others.

---

2. See Hebrews 8:10.
3. 2 Corinthians 1:20
4. See Leviticus 25:8–12.

We also have a posture of hope. Christians do not dismiss nor downplay all that is broken in the world but recognize that the land of exile can be a scary and fearful place. But instead of falling into dread and despair, we can experience hope. This hope is not wishful thinking that perhaps one day things might get better, but a certainty that evil will be eradicated and all things will be made new when Jesus returns in victory and glory. Hallelujah, amen!

DISCUSSION *10 MINUTES*

What would our Christian community be like if we all more fully embraced a "proud versus humble" mentality instead of a "good versus bad" mentality? What would it take to get us there?

Share a story of a time when you encountered someone "greater"—more beautiful, more powerful, more successful—than you. Where were you and how did you respond? Why do you think you responded in this way?

PRAYER: INVOCATION, CONFESSION, AND PETITION

20 MINUTES

In this chapter, we see what conviction of sin looks like in the way Daniel prays. Read back over Daniel's prayer in verses 4–19. Notice that he prays using invocation, confession, and petition:

- **Invocation:** he calls upon the Lord (vv. 4–5)
- **Confession:** he admits sin and wrongdoing (vv. 6–15)
- **Petition:** he pleads for God's mercy, asking him to do something (vv. 16–29)

Here is an example of what this looks like:

> ***(Invocation)*** *Lord, you are a holy God through whom we are saved by grace alone. You are perfectly righteous and just.* ***(Confession)*** *But I confess to you that often, in my pride, I think there are sinners who are worse than I am, and I fall into the thinking that I am accepted and favored by you because I am better and more faithful than others. Forgive me—I have forgotten the gospel!* ***(Petition)*** *Help*

me to not only grasp your grace but to joyfully repent. I am reminded of what Jack Miller has said: "Cheer up, you are far worse than you think," and "Cheer up! God's grace is greater than you've ever dared hope!"[5]

Here's another example of a prayer that includes invocation, confession, and petition:

(Invocation) *Lord, you are sovereign, and you love my kids far more than I do. You know what's best for them, and you care about their hearts and their needs.* ***(Confession)*** *I confess to you my anxiety and desire for control over them. I want to fix them; I feel like I need to step in because I think you are too slow to respond. O Lord, forgive me of my sin, and forgive me for doubting your love and care.* ***(Petition)*** *Help me to rest in your love and wisdom, not only for my life but also for the lives of my children. When I question your love, help me to behold what you did at the cross out of love for me so that I could become a child of God! Change my heart from doubting you to trusting you. If you did not withhold your own Son, how will you not also graciously give us all things in your great wisdom and love!*[6]

For this exercise, you are going to write out your own prayer incorporating invocation, confession, and petition. You won't be asked to share your specific prayer with your group, but you will talk about your experience of including these three elements in your prayer.

---

5. Quoted in Michael A. Graham, *Cheer Up! The Life and Ministry of Jack Miller* (P&R Publishing, 2020), xiv.
6. Romans 8:32

Write out your own prayer, as we live in exile.

Invocation: Remember who God is and what he has done. Call upon his name.

Confession: Admit your sin, confessing how you have fallen short by compromising in exile or looking to the comforts and promises of the culture for rescue.

Petition: Ask God for mercy and deliverance. Remember that he has rescued you through Jesus's work and that he has given you his Spirit.

When your group is ready to regather, discuss your experience of incorporating these three elements into a prayer. How does this differ from your usual way of praying?

Anytime we try something new, it can feel a little clunky or forced; that's to be expected. Rather than focusing on the awkward part, discuss with your group what these elements added to your prayer. What is beneficial about them?

WRAP-UP AND PRAYER *10 MINUTES*

With invocation, confession, and petition in mind, have someone close your time together in prayer.

Lesson

10

THE END

BIG IDEA

As the Lord continues to give Daniel visions about the future, what awaits is ultimate vindication, judgment, and restoration. Although we do not know when that will be, Christians ought to live with this glorious end in mind.

BIBLE CONVERSATION *20 MINUTES*

This lesson is aptly called "The End," not only because it's the final one in our study, but also because it focuses on the time of the end of this world. This lesson covers three chapters, which essentially make up one unit, one vision.

Since this is a longer text, we are going to approach it a little differently. In the Bible Conversation, your group will read and discuss chapter 10. Then the article will draw out a main point from each of the last three chapters. Finally, we will wrap up our last lesson by reflecting on key themes from the whole book of Daniel, tying them to Jesus, who alone enables us to stand firm in adversity.

Begin by having someone read **Daniel 10**. Then discuss the following questions:

As we come to the end of the book, Daniel is spent, his strength depleted. How would you describe your emotional response to the time we've spent together looking at life in exile?

What do you find particularly strengthening or encouraging about Daniel's interaction with the angelic messenger (the man clothed in linen)?

****

Now read the following article. Take turns reading it aloud, switching readers at each paragraph break. Then discuss the questions that follow the article.

Lesson

FINAL ENCOURAGEMENT TO STAND FIRM IN ADVERSITY

5 MINUTES

Living in exile, we see or experience things like catastrophic world events, difficult relationships, and personal suffering, and at times it can feel like the world is falling apart. How do we stand firm in adversity? The closing chapters of Daniel show us a way.

ENGAGE THE SPIRITUAL BATTLE IN PRAYER (DANIEL 10)

In Daniel 10 we see the connection between prayer and the unseen reality of spiritual battles. Daniel is heavy-hearted over the revelation he has been given. An angelic being comes to strengthen Daniel and speak words of love, peace, and courage. He tells Daniel, "Your words have been heard, and I have come because of your words" (v. 12). What's implied is that if Daniel had not prayed, the angel would not have come. But because Daniel did pray, the angel came to him. That's the power of prayer!

The angel also mentions the deep spiritual warfare taking place in Persia and tells Daniel that he has been fighting there. This encounter with the angel opens our eyes to the reality that spiritual battles are taking place that we cannot see. If Daniel prayed and angels went into battle, and if there were strongholds in Persia and Greece in Daniel's day, we should recognize that there are strongholds impacting our lives, our country, and our world today, and that our prayers are powerful. As we pray, we are engaging with a deep, unseen spiritual realm and reality.

GAIN PERSPECTIVE BY FOCUSING ON GOD'S SOVEREIGNTY (DANIEL 11)

In chapter 11 the heavenly messenger speaks to Daniel of earthly nations and rulers battling for power and control. We see over and over that kingdoms and rulers come and go. They make noise and bring hardship and suffering for a time, but their quest for lasting power and control is ultimately futile.

The futility of earthly kings and kingdoms is a comfort to God's people, who are often caught in the crossfire. We can grow discouraged by the evil taking place in the world, but God's Word reminds us that it will not last. And any hope we place in earthly rulers and kingdoms is a false hope. As God's people, we are challenged to put our hope instead in the Lord and his good and lasting kingdom.

As earthly kings and kingdoms rise and fall, God is in complete control. Evil empires do not last. They will not have the final say. When it feels like the world is crumbling, Daniel 11 gives us the ability to recognize the futility of the nations and to trust in God's sovereignty over them all.

KNOW THAT SUFFERING AND EVIL WILL NOT TRIUMPH, BUT GOD WILL (DANIEL 12)

In his commentary on Daniel, Dale Davis talks about how we can have *security*, *certainty*, and *tenacity* as we endure to the end.[1] Using these three terms, let us look at how Daniel 12 connects to our lives today:

1. Knowing that the Lord will win, God's people can have *security* when things are at their worst.

> "But at that time your people shall be delivered, everyone whose name shall be found written in the book. And many of those who sleep in the dust of the earth shall awake, some to everlasting life, and some to shame and everlasting contempt. And those who are wise shall shine like the brightness of the sky above; and those who turn many to righteousness, like the stars forever and ever." (Daniel 12:1–3)

There is deep comfort knowing that God's people will not ultimately perish; rather, they will shine like stars forever and ever. We have this eternal security because Jesus has gone into exile before us and returned victorious over sin and death. One day he will return and eradicate all evil once and for all.

2. Knowing that the Lord will win, God's people can have *certainty* in the most difficult of trials.

> And I heard the man clothed in linen, who was above the waters of the stream; he raised his right hand and his left hand toward heaven and swore by him who lives forever that it would be for a time, times, and half a time, and that when the shattering of the power of the holy

---

1. Dale Davis, *The Message of Daniel* (IVP Press, 2013), 161–69.

> people comes to an end all these things would be finished. (Daniel 12:7)

The act of raising the right and left hands toward heaven indicates that an oath is being made. The angel swears by the eternal God that suffering, evil, and persecution will not last forever; their time is limited. We who are living after the resurrection of Christ know that God has already won the victory. Jesus was raised as the first fruit of the new creation, and he has promised to return. He has also given us the additional guarantee of our inheritance, the promised Holy Spirit,[2] who empowers us to live with hope even in the most difficult of trials.

3. Knowing that the Lord will win, God's people can have *tenacity* instead of wilting under fear or pressure.

> "But go your way till the end. And you shall rest and shall stand in your allotted place at the end of the days." (Daniel 12:13)

In this last verse, Daniel is essentially told, "Knowing all that has been revealed to you, continue to live by faith in exile. Stand firm in adversity." And this servant of God, who has endured long years in exile, is given the promise of rest.

Like Daniel, we are to continue to live by faith in exile, knowing all that we've read and reflected on in the book of Daniel and how it points us to Jesus, the greater Daniel, who entered into our exile to bring us home.

So rest in God's faithfulness to you. Come to him in prayer, for he hears you and fights for you. Keep an eternal perspective: Kings and kingdoms come and go, but God rules forever. Stand firm in adversity, knowing that the Lord will triumph in the end. Christ will return and bring us home from exile. Amen.

---

2. Ephesians 1:13–14

DISCUSSION *10 MINUTES*

How does it challenge or encourage you to think of prayer as engaging in spiritual battle?

Which of these seems like your greatest need for growth as you live in exile—security, certainty, or tenacity? How does your time in Daniel speak to this need?

Lesson

GOING FORWARD

20 MINUTES

Throughout this study, we have seen how Daniel lives by faith in an extreme situation. He has pointed us to Jesus, who is with us even in exile. And Daniel's example gives us handrails to guide our own steps as we, too, live by faith in exile. Together we'll seek God's wisdom and grace to live faithfully until Jesus returns to usher in the ultimate homecoming.

This exercise is a time to think back on how God has given you wisdom and grace from your study of Daniel, and to consider how you'll go forward as you live in exile until Christ's return. You'll work on your own to think back on all you've learned. Then the group will come back together to share.

Each box below mentions one broad topic the study has addressed. Think of something about that topic that you have learned, come to appreciate better, or become more confident about. Check the one that applies to you, and then fill in the box with a few details.

Something about **God's sovereign power** that I have . . .
- ☐ Learned
- ☐ Come to better appreciate
- ☐ Become more confident about

Something about **Babylon—its influence or its futility—**that I have . . .
- ☐ Learned
- ☐ Come to better appreciate
- ☐ Become more confident about

Something about **Christ's victory and return** that I have . . .
- ☐ Learned
- ☐ Come to better appreciate
- ☐ Become more confident about

Something about **living by faith in exile** that I have . . .
- ☐ Learned
- ☐ Come to better appreciate
- ☐ Become more confident about

When the group is ready, share and explain some of your responses.

Then discuss these general questions:

How have you become more confident of God's power and victory?

How has the life of Daniel or the apocalyptic messages he received changed some aspect of your life in exile?

WRAP-UP AND PRAYER *10 MINUTES*

Pray for one another about the specific ways you want to live by faith in exile. If your group is going to keep meeting after you finish this study, you might discuss your plans.

LEADER'S NOTES

LESSON 1: THE EXILE

Jehoiakim, the king of Judah, was not a good king; he did many egregiously horrible things. Instead of following the example of his father, Josiah, who feared God, Jehoiakim abused his own people and murdered God's servants (Jeremiah 26:20–23). In 2 Kings 23:37, the writer summarizes Jehoiakim's reign: "And he did what was evil in the sight of the LORD."

Not only are God's people taken into exile, but the temple vessels are taken as well (v. 2). The removal of these vessels is sad because they were made to be used for worship in God's holy house, and they are now being moved to the Babylonian temple. Placing them in the Babylonian place of worship is a form of mocking: "Our god is greater than your god!" That the destruction of Judah goes so far as to mock Israel's God reflects the tragic nature of Israel's disobedience and sin. And yet in the midst of all this, God is very much in control.

Even here in the beginning of the book of Daniel, we have a picture of the end. Daniel was in Babylon until the first year of King Cyrus (v. 21). King Cyrus was the king of Persia who conquered Babylon. Mighty Babylon, a kingdom that had defeated Israel with power and strength, is overthrown during Daniel's lifetime. Babylon is gone, yet Daniel is still present. Even in exile, God is faithfully at work, and his reign will not be thwarted. We'll see this theme continue to play out throughout the book of Daniel.

LESSON 2: THE DREAM

There are at least two possible ways to understand Daniel's interpretation of Nebuchadnezzar's dream (2:36–45). One way of understanding the statue is linear or sequential: It's a message to Nebuchadnezzar (the head of gold) that his kingdom won't last forever. As history reveals, Persia (silver) would come next, then the Greeks (bronze), then the Romans (iron, which was powerful but unstable). That's when Jesus would come—the One who has more power than all these other kingdoms.

Another way to understand the statue is this: Instead of referring to a sequence of specific kingdoms, the statue is describing the *nature* of Babylon and all successive kingdoms and empires. The effect of sin is that it degrades, causing division and breakdown. Without God, kingdoms do not "advance" and reach a golden age of society, when everything gets better and more wonderful and glorious. In fact, the opposite happens because of sin. Kingdoms rise and fall, dominating and crushing others, leading to instability and division in human history and society.

Either understanding of the meaning of the statue points to the important climax: A stone is coming that will destroy these kingdoms (vv. 34–35). And the God of heaven will set up a new kingdom, an everlasting kingdom, that shall stand forever (v. 44).

LESSON 3: THE FIERY FURNACE

This is a powerful story of God's deliverance. Pay attention to how people in your group respond to God's deliverance of Daniel's three friends. Yes, God has the power to deliver us from scary and hard situations, and we certainly need to pray for that; when you're in the fire, you pray. But this is not a promise that God will deliver us every single time. God is not a genie who shows up to deliver us when we snap our fingers.

Some people might think, *If I just have enough faith, then God will deliver me*. Others might think, *If God's not delivering me, then he must not love me*. These are lies.

To counter both lies, look at Jesus in the garden of Gethsemane.

Lie #1: *If I have enough faith, God must deliver me.* Did Jesus have enough faith? Was he lacking anything? Did he not fully trust his Abba, Father? Jesus loved, obeyed, and trusted his Father perfectly. Even so, the Father did not "remove this cup" from Jesus (Luke 22:42).

Lie #2: *God must not love me if he doesn't deliver me.* Again, look at Jesus. We know that Jesus is the beloved Son, yet God doesn't deliver him from his suffering on the cross.

So how can we find hope and comfort when we're in the fire? By looking at Jesus. See Jesus going through the ultimate fire for us on the cross, taking our judgment so that we can be eternally safe. As we go through fiery trials in exile today, truly there is another in the fire with us: the risen Jesus.

LESSON 4: THE HUMBLED KING

There are a couple of wisdom areas you'll want to have in mind as your group discusses Daniel 4.

First, you'll want to be alert to the distinction between *good* pride and *bad* pride. The Bible talks about a good kind of pride. In 2 Corinthians 7:4, the apostle Paul says to the Corinthians, "I am acting with great boldness toward you; I have great pride in you; I am filled with comfort. In all our affliction, I am overflowing with joy." As a spiritual father, Paul loves his spiritual children and takes pride in them. There's a good kind of pride that reflects love and affection.

But there's also bad pride. Bad pride is a focus on the self, resulting in self-absorption and self-exaltation. This form of pride causes a person to look down upon others, feeling smug and superior. We see this bad pride in Nebuchadnezzar, and this is what lies in our hearts as well. Proverbs 11:2 says, "When pride comes, then comes disgrace, but with the humble is wisdom." This verse comes to life in the account of Nebuchadnezzar. His pride leads to disgrace. But when he is humbled by God, Nebuchadnezzar learns wisdom and praises God's greatness and power, not his own.

Second, God's warning is meant to protect us and awaken us.

Nebuchadnezzar had great power and took pride in all that he had accomplished. Such power and pride led to an unrighteous life that oppressed others. So God sends Nebuchadnezzar another dream that greatly troubles him, and Daniel interprets the dream for the king. Ultimately, the purpose of the dream (and Daniel's interpretation) is to warn Nebuchadnezzar, to protect him from himself and the deadly sin of pride.

In what ways might God be sending us a warning today to protect us and awaken us from the illusion of our pride? Perhaps there are areas of sin in our lives that we downplay or dismiss, and God provides a "dream" (something that alarms us) or a "Daniel" (someone who confronts us). Will we respond in humility or in pride?

Knowing that our hearts are prone to wander, may we pray, "God, make me receptive to you so that I might turn to you and acknowledge my need for your correction, healing, mercy, and grace in my life."

LESSON 5: THE WRITING ON THE WALL

A few pieces of history will be helpful for this lesson.

Belshazzar is the last king of Babylon, and the events in this chapter take place on the final evening of his rule, on the cusp of the overthrow of Babylon by the Medo-Persian Empire.

The ancient Greek historians Heraclitus and Xenophon give their account of how Babylon fell. Babylon was considered an impenetrable fortress. It had walls that were twenty-five feet thick—who could break through? It had walls that were forty feet high—who could go over them? In addition, the Euphrates River flowed through Babylon, so they had fresh water, and they had stockpiled a great deal of food. Thus, even if they were under siege, they were not worried.

Unbeknownst to Belshazzar, the Medo-Persian army had dug a trench and siphoned the water of the Euphrates off to a marsh. This lowered the water level in the river to their waists. On this particular night, a few soldiers went underneath the fortress of Babylon and broke through, killing the king. Belshazzar and his kingdom were no more.

Regarding the phrase "that very night" (v. 30): Where have you heard this before? In the parable that Jesus tells in Luke 12, the rich fool finds security in his wealth and thinks, *Eat, drink, and be merry, for no matter what happens in the future, I am secure*. But God says to him, "You fool. *This very night* your life will be demanded from you. Then who will get what you have prepared for yourself?" (v. 20 NIV, emphasis added). What happens to Belshazzar is essentially the Old Testament version of the parable of the rich fool.

What about the words that prophesied this downfall? The words that appear on the wall are: *Mene*, *Mene*, *Tekel*, and *Parsin* (Daniel 5:25). These words are Aramaic, a language that doesn't have any vowels. The words are written in one stream, with no separation between them, so they would have been hard to understand. But these words have to do with weights and scales: *mene* signifies "numbered," *tekel* signifies "weighed," and *parsin* or *peres* signifies "divided" (vv. 26–28).

LESSON 6: THE LION'S DEN

There is a unique dynamic about the Christian faith that's going to repel some people. Many people don't believe that humans are broken and sinful, unable to save themselves. The idea that none of us are by nature good and we need Jesus to save us from our sin is offensive. The world often says, "How dare you tell me this? Who are you to say we are all under God's wrath? That's just awful. It sounds so arrogant to say Jesus alone can save."

And yet there's something very attractive about having a relationship with God. King Darius is attracted to Daniel. It's as if he is saying, "Daniel, there's something about your faith that impacts the way you live and work with integrity. I can see you're not living for yourself and seeking your own self-promotion." Living by faith in exile is like a magnet—it repels some and attracts others.

A further note on how to engage the world as exiles: God's people are to be like salt. Jesus in the Sermon on the Mount says, "You are the salt of the earth" (Matthew 5:13). In the book of Daniel, we see Daniel living as salt in Babylon.

One of the dangers for Christians today is to stay completely unengaged and removed from the world. But our passage is saying that, like Daniel, we are called to engage as salt. And salt has no purpose if it stays in the saltshaker.

In the ancient Near East, when, where, and why did they use salt? It was used as a preservative for food to keep it from spoiling. So what are those spots, those pockets and spaces, in our city and our world that are messy, spoiling, and difficult? What does it mean for God's people to be salt, moving toward and not running away from those places?

One last comment regarding the miracle in the lion's den: Some who deny the miraculous nature of this account suggest that Daniel was unharmed because the lions were old or because they had been fed beforehand and weren't hungry. No. Daniel was supernaturally protected. God made the lions do a form of fasting while Daniel was down in the pit with them. Notice that afterward the lions devoured others (v. 24). What we see here is that the living God whom Daniel served is the ultimate Deliverer!

LESSON 7: THE FOUR BEASTS

Here are some notes on how the imagery of Daniel 7 is often interpreted. Guide your group to use this in ways that build your understanding of this chapter, but take care not to get so caught up in the details that you lose sight of the big picture.

In verse 2, "the four winds of heaven" refers to the north, south, east, and west—all the ends of the earth. The winds are stirring the great sea, which in the ancient Near East represented chaotic forces—darkness, confusion, evil.

There are various ways people interpret the meaning of the four beasts.

One of the ways to understand the four beasts in verses 1–18 is that they represent successive kingdoms from history. Some suggest that the lion with eagles' wings is Babylon, the bear is the Medes, the leopard is Persia, and the ten-horned beast is Greece. The fourth beast seems to fit Greece because the Greeks had great power under Alexander the Great, and then in the second century BC a "little horn"-like figure named Antiochus Epiphanes rose to power. Antiochus Epiphanes was incredibly violent, persecuting God's people in a horrific way.

Another reading of the four beasts is this: the first beast refers to Babylon, the bear to the Medes and Persians together (the Medo-Persian Empire), the swift leopard to Greece (due to Alexander the Great's quick rise to power), and the ten-horned beast to Rome—a power like no other.

A third possible interpretation is the one referenced in the article. These four beasts symbolically represent the nature of all earthly kingdoms and how the nature of sin escalates in intensity and evil.

Remember, the point is not to get caught up in specific details. What this vision does tell us is that different beastly kings and kingdoms will always arise, attacking and bringing harm to God's world and God's people. But their oppression is limited by God, and God will tame and overthrow such beasts by his mighty power.

LESSON 8: THE RAM AND THE GOAT

Here's a high-level summary of how this prophecy might be understood historically.

Daniel is in exile, and Babylon is in power. This prophecy tells us that after Babylon, the Medo-Persian kingdom will rise to power. It will seem very powerful, like a ram. But then a goat will come along and overthrow it, and the goat is Greece.

As we look back in history, we can see that the horned goat that defeats the Medo-Persian Empire seems to be Alexander the Great. Once he passes away, four other horns pop up, signifying the four kingdoms that will be established within the Greek empire. And one of them, the little horn, will speak with great pride and will persecute God's people.

Again, as we look back in history, biblical scholars suggest that this little horn is Antiochus Epiphanes. Around 170–160 BC, he persecuted God's people, who had returned to Jerusalem from exile and had built a temple for the worship of Yahweh. Antiochus Epiphanes profaned the temple, putting an image of Zeus inside it. He called on God's people to worship Zeus, and if they refused, they would be killed.

Interestingly, the second part of his name, Epiphanes, means "God manifests." This leader (the little horn) was declaring, "I am God-like, like Zeus." This boastful ruler slaughtered thousands of people because of their refusal to reject the true God and his law. And the things that Antiochus Epiphanes did (such as placing the statue of Zeus in God's house) led to the Maccabean revolt and to Hanukkah.

Some might think, *Wait a minute, that's really specific prophecy; it can't be true.* In an attempt to "make sense" of the specificity of this prophecy, some think this chapter was written many years after Daniel (around the 150s BC) by someone using Daniel as a pseudonym, making such historical connections after the fact. Christians, however, do not have a problem with the specific nature of the prophecy recorded in this chapter. A supernatural God who knows all things and transcends time and space can certainly provide a specific and detailed account of the future from a human, time-bound perspective!

In addition, many Bible scholars have examined the linguistic features of Daniel 8. Their examination has led them to conclude that this chapter could not have been written in the 150s BC, because the style of Aramaic and Hebrew that appears in it was only used centuries earlier. Linguistic evidence indicates that this chapter was written around 550 BC, which is around the time when Daniel was alive.

LESSON 9: THE PRAYER AND SEVENTY WEEKS

As noted in the main part of the study, the best way to read the prophetic portions of Daniel is as a big picture book instead of as a puzzle to be solved. This doesn't mean that we shouldn't seek to understand what is being said, but rather, we should not get so caught up in trying to decipher the details that we miss the overall message the book of Daniel is trying to convey: God reigns. And because God reigns, we can stand firm in adversity.

It is important to keep this in mind as we come to a section of Daniel that is often debated: the seventy weeks.

How long are the time periods described in Daniel 9?

The "seventy weeks" in Daniel 9:24 is likely not a literal but an overall symbolic period of time. Compare this to Matthew 18:21–22, when

Peter asks Jesus whether he has to forgive his brother "as many as seven times," and Jesus responds, "I do not say to you seven times, but seventy-seven [or seventy times seven] times." Jesus is not being literal here; he's not saying it's just 490 times, and after that, you no longer forgive. Rather, the number seven is symbolic and represents completion, perfection, or wholeness in the Bible. The point is that in Christ, God's people are to *always* forgive. There is no cap or end limit. Similarly, the "seventy" in Daniel 9 is symbolic.

The angel Gabriel tells Daniel that there will be a decree of seventy weeks "to finish the transgression, to put an end to sin, and to atone for iniquity, to bring in everlasting righteousness, to seal both vision and prophet, and to anoint a most holy place" (v. 24). The seventy weeks is broken down into seven weeks (a relatively restricted time), sixty-two weeks (a relatively extended time), and the last week (a climactic finale).[1]

There are various interpretations as to what the seven weeks, the sixty-two weeks, and the final week refer to. One possible suggestion is that the first seven weeks refer to the time between Cyrus's edict, which allowed God's people to return from exile, to the period of Ezra, when Jerusalem is rebuilt and restored. The sixty-two weeks would then be the longer period from the time of Ezra to the coming of Christ, which is characterized as "a troubled time" (v. 25). Seven weeks plus sixty-two weeks takes us to sixty-nine weeks.

The final week is unique in that it is the seventieth week. As already mentioned, in the Bible the number seven signifies completion and wholeness. With this symbolic understanding in mind, various biblical scholars suggest that the final "seventieth" week is unique in that its focus is not on a duration of time (like the previous two) but rather on the ultimate and complete time, the climactic finale of God's victory over worldly kings and kingdoms that have defied God.

---

1. Dale Davis, *The Message of Daniel* (IVP Press, 2013), 134.

This "week," then, would be the period between Christ's first coming and his return.

The *he* at the beginning of verse 27 could be referring to Jesus: "And *he* shall make a strong covenant with many for one week, and for half of the week he shall put an end to sacrifice and offering" (emphasis added).

The "end to sacrifice" in that verse could be referring to Christ's death on the cross, which puts an end to the sacrificial system, as we read in Hebrews 8 and 10.[2]

The half a week in verse 27 is interesting. Since one week consists of 7 days, half a week consists of 3.5 days. Again, without trying to get too caught up in the details, the mention of half a week could mean that the work of Jesus is still unfinished: there's still another half week that remains.

The book of Daniel does not tell us about the latter "half of the week," or 3.5 days, but, interestingly, it's possible that the book of Revelation picks up where Daniel left off:

- Revelation 11:2–3 (42 months = 1260 days = around 3.5 years)
- Revelation 13:5 (42 months = around 3.5 years)

The "3.5" period of time mentioned in Revelation could then mean that the final "half week" takes place between Christ's death on the cross and his future return in glory (or possibly between AD 70 and Christ's return).

2. Jesus draws upon Daniel 9 when he speaks of the abomination of desolation in Mark 13:14–23; many scholars believe Jesus is referring to the destruction of the temple in Jerusalem that takes place in AD 70.

LESSON 10: THE END

Who is the "man clothed in linen" (10:5)?

Some commentaries think that Daniel is seeing a vision of Jesus (v. 5) because the book of Revelation describes Jesus in a similar way. However, it's more likely that this is an angelic being with great splendor, dressed in armor and ready for battle.

The reason this explanation is more likely is found in verses 13–14. These verses refer to the prince of the kingdom of Persia, who is not a person but a supernatural being. The speaker says that this prince of Persia withstood him for twenty-one days, and the angel Michael had to come and help him. Because the man clothed in linen needed the angel Michael's help to prevail, we have good reason to believe that he is not Jesus. In the Bible, when Jesus is revealed in his glory, everyone falls to the ground and is powerless, and Jesus absolutely needs no help! Similarly, in other places where the Bible shows God engaging in battle, it's over very quickly (as in his defeat of the beast in Daniel 7:11). God wins, crushing his enemies, and that is that.

How Do We Engage in Spiritual Warfare?

This lesson briefly discusses the reality of spiritual warfare and our engagement in these battles through prayer. Now, Christians face two temptations here: to casually dismiss spiritual warfare or to get overly caught up in it.

A word to those who are prone to dismiss or downplay the supernatural: The Bible highlights the *reality* of supernatural forces (Ephesians 6:10–12). If you do not recognize that reality, you will be ineffective in your walk and witness for Christ as you're living in exile. Daniel 10 is a wake-up call: We are to fight on our knees. God is at work, and he responds to our prayers.

A word to those who might be overly caught up in the supernatural: Yes, Daniel 10 highlights the importance of prayer and doing battle spiritually. Engaging in spiritual warfare is an important part of a praying life. But couple that with how Daniel 9 highlights the prayer of repentance. Prayer is not just for engaging in a spiritual battle; prayer entails communing with God, delighting in God, confessing our sins to God, and offering supplication to God! In other words, prayer is covenantal. It is relational. Prayer flows out of our relationship with God through Jesus. Therefore, it involves all aspects of our covenant relationship with God—whether that's waging spiritual battle, interceding, trusting, resting, praising, or confessing.